1001 Arabian Nightmares

A collection of short stories

1001 Arabian Nightmares

A collection of short stories

Narendra Simone

ISBN 978-1-105-48277-9

المصائب لا تأتي فرادى

Disasters do not come one by one.

An Arabic Proverb

Praise for Narendra's Books:

"Reading *Desert Song* is what I imagine a few evenings to be like of listening to a master story teller take us through the descent of Beowulf. Medieval in its proportions, gruesome in its verity, raw in its necessity, *Desert Song* exposes the sinister triangulations of politics, religion, and law in a world wrought with dark forces. Our hero, Matt Slater, witnesses unimaginable crimes in his desperate search for a lost child. Startling ironies erupt on each page as Simone's first thriller hurtles us through a journey both disturbing and authentic. Before you read any other book on the Taliban, read this book first." -- Almeda Glenn Miller, author of *"Tiger Dreams"*

"In his riveting story, The Last Goodbye, Narendra Simone skillfully portrays the soul of a mother/son relationship in a culture that remains an enigma to so many of us." – Mike Sirota, author of *"Fire Dance"* and *"The Burning Ground"*.

PROLOGUE

Joe and Bill, newly arrived expats from their company in the USA, walk into the Hemingway Bar at the Hilton Hotel in Abu Dhabi and meet with their agent Mr. Kumar, an expat from India living in Abu Dhabi for the past ten years…

Mr. Kumar: Welcoming you to Abu Dhabi. Would you be drinking beer?

Joe: That is what people do when they go to a bar. Yeah, we'd be drinking beer.

Mr. Kumar: This here is like Hotel California, *'You can checkout anytime you like, but you can never leave.'* You can drink but then you should not go out, and must sleep in this hotel. You see, no one is allowed on the streets or even in a taxi with alcohol in their blood, the law of the land.

Bill: You kidding me? And here I thought it was my lucky day. I found a five-dollar bill lying on the floor on my way in.

Mr. Kumar: Like everyone who came the same way, I saw it too. But in this country you don't pick up money off the ground or you could be charged with stealing and punishment for that is chopping off your hands.

Bill (covertly dropping five-dollar bill out of his pocket and onto the floor): I didn't say I picked it up. Give us two beers with whisky chasers and while you are at it, book us two rooms, too.

Joe (to Mr. Kumar): With all these strict laws, how have you managed to survive all these years?

Mr. Kumar (grinning): Easily. No taxes, plenty of sunshine, and no cows on the roads, *'such a lovely place....'*

Bill (stopping Mr. Kumar as he breaks into 'Hotel California' again): Wait a minute—it's all a bit weird. People put up with such strict laws just to make tax-free money?

Mr. Kumar (perplexed): Isn't that why you're here? Do you think you're on some kind of Arabian adventure? You know, *'On a dark desert highway, cool wind in my hair..."*

Bill (exasperated): For crying out loud, enough of the Eagles, okay? We're here because our corporation is interested in investing in this region to help build the local economy.

Mr. Kumar (laughing and others in the bar smirking): These people here are paying you tax-free dollars because they're interested in your technology and not in you. You have already done enough damage to this region.

Joe (intrigued): What damage?

Mr. Kumar (after ordering a second beer): Middle East spring, Iraq war, Egyptian freedom, and Libya revolution. And if that was not enough, an earthquake in Iran and flooding in Yemen.

Joe (amused and cancelling Kumar's order of beer and ordering a bottle of wine): Earthquake and flooding, what has that to do with us?

Mr. Kumar (first responding to the offer of wine): '*Please bring me some wine, we haven't had that spirit here since nineteen sixty-nine….*' What? You don't know? It is the FBI. They do all this stuff, including earthquakes and flooding. People here totally believe in this. Your technology is fantastic. How do you do all these things?

Bill (laughing): We don't. We're a God-fearing nation and do not interfere in divine acts of justice.

Mr. Kumar: Oh, we know that too. That is why God is punishing you by getting Sarah Palin into US politics and the meek are inheriting the White House.

Bill: What? That doesn't even make sense. If you dislike the US so much then why have you been working for us for so long?

Mr. Kumar (sighing): Beastly greed, pure greed, you know, money, green cards, hamburgers, Wal-Mart, Disneyland…ah, like they say, *'They stab it with their steely knives, but they just can't kill the beast.'* It is the greed.

Bartender (showing a bottle of wine): Here is our special house red, Chateau Ksara from the Bekaa Valley of Lebanon.

Bill (shaking head): Forget the wine, okay? Let us have the beer.

Bartender: I could offer an Indian wine. I know Mr. Kumar likes it. They are on special today, buy one, and get one free?

Bill & Joe (in unison): Stick with the beer, would you?

Note: The above conversation should set the scene for you to expect some humor in what follows, but please do not expect logic.

CONTENTS

1

THE YELLOW SAND ROAD

I'll tell you something, but you have to promise to keep it a secret. A woman can use both the left and the right side of her brain simultaneously. This makes women naturals at negotiating. Trust me when I tell you that against women's shrewdness and cunning, men have as much chance as lambs in a slaughterhouse. I may have held executive positions in major corporations and negotiated some tough contracts, but all that skill and experience is useless when I have to negotiate with my lady for something as simple as an extra five minutes in front of the TV.

Case in point: Not long ago, I was a senior executive at a major pipeline services company in downtown Calgary, Alberta, Canada. One Friday evening, I finished a grueling day at the office and drove home in my brand-new, luxury Grand Cherokee (compliments of said company). I pulled into the attached, triple-car garage of our four-bedroom house with built-in gymnasium and hot tub, located on a hill overlooking the Rockies. Yes, life was good.

I knew my lady had gone on a shopping spree and wouldn't be home until late that evening. As I entered the house, I looked forward to an evening spent in front of the TV. To my amazement, I found her sitting in the lounge, wearing very little and holding a bottle of Prestige de Grand Bateau Bordeaux. She poured me a generous glass of the red wine and gave me a smile.

Now, you may think that I suffer from paranoia, but I knew *that* smile. It meant— *Come, tangle yourself in my web.* I nervously swallowed a mouthful of wine, smoothed my necktie, and sat uneasily on the edge of the sofa.

She said, "Why so far away? Come sit next to me." She paused as she took an intentionally slow sip from her glass. A faint smile of invincibility was flickering on her lips. "I have something to tell you. We are moving to the Middle East. I've been contracted as an emergency physician in Abu Dhabi, and it pays more than what you make here. So, please come with me?"

Now does that sound like an invitation, or a threat to you? See, you're confused too.

To me, it sounded more like a challenge—*Come on, give me a reason to cry so I can make you feel guilty.*

Well, I had to defend my position, as God made men foolish for the enjoyment of women, so I articulated, "But we're happy here." I saw her smile dissolving but I persevered, "I've a great job, we have a great house, and you live a life of luxury while I work. Why do you want to change all that?"

"It's bloody cold here," she retorted and then she played the trump card that literally stopped all arguments, "and there are no palm trees."

"And it's rather hot over there in the Middle East." I tried to use her logic in reverse and gulped wine, hoping that intoxication would build my inner strength.

"Why are you always so difficult?" Her brow narrowing implying it was time for me to surrender. She continued, "Why don't you support me? We'll have a company car and a house, and they'll pay for our vacation and utilities. Isn't that great?"

I must admit, it sounded wonderful. But the Middle East was no Canada. I'd heard that people there were lashed in public for traffic violations and had their hands amputated for minor offenses like pick pocketing, not that I had any such plans. And they harassed everyone who looked like they came from America, Americans and Canadians alike, because they believed that everyone from America belonged to the CIA. I don't think our foreign ministry has done a good job of educating Arab states on the differences between Canada and the United States—such as its being a different country, eh. They believe we are all part of the big ol' USA—but then, there might be some truth in that.

I sat contemplating these tales for a few moments, delicately holding my wine glass by its long elegant stem with my pinky extended out, when, taking my momentary silence as submission, she added, "And guess what? They have no income tax there."

That was it. I was really getting sick of playing the catch-up game with Revenue Canada, and knew I would never win. I almost spilled my wine I stood up so fast. "What the hell are we waiting for?" I cried. "Let's go to Abu Dhabi." A few months later, I'd resigned from my job, we'd sold our house, and we were off to see the sheikh, the wonderful sheikh of Abu Dhabi.

One sunny day, like all other days, we sat admiring the ocean from the balcony of our complimentary two-bedroom apartment while drinking copious quantities of red wine bought with my lady's tax-free income. Granted, it wasn't a sprawling house overlooking the Canadian Rockies. But hey, it was free. And the ocean was a true azure blue, so I decided I could get used to this lifestyle.

Abu Dhabi City, the capital of Abu Dhabi emirate, is the largest of the seven emirates of the United Arab Emirates, commonly known as the UAE. It includes Abu Dhabi, Dubai, Fujairah, Khor Fakkan, Ras Al Khaimah, Ajman, and Sharjah. Doesn't that sound better than Moose Jaw? The UAE, a member country of the Gulf Cooperation Council that also includes Saudi Arabia, Kuwait, Bahrain, Qatar and Oman, borders Saudi Arabia in the south and southwest, Oman in the east, Qatar in the west, and the Arabian Gulf in the north. Well, one does feel surrounded and in the middle of the, hmm, 'The Middle East.'

In Abu Dhabi you feel like you are living in a tiny, artificially created sheikhdom surrounded by the mighty and fierce Middle Eastern powers. Talk about being in a hot spot, and of course, one needs a lot to drink here— and I don't mean just water.

I heard that during the Gulf War (the first one, not the sequel), when Saddam

Hussein was planning his invasion of Kuwait and Saudi Arabia, he was asked how big an army he would need to attack the UAE. He replied that a mere fax message ought to do it. And he wasn't kidding (but I am). Small they might be but the emirates are a shining example of modern and model states.

I was astounded to learn that in Abu Dhabi and most of the other emirates, consumption of alcohol is not prohibited, as it is in Saudi Arabia, Iran, and Iraq. Here we have nightclubs, bars, and even cheap Russian cabarets. Mind you, there are only two liquor stores in the whole city, and to buy alcohol you need a permit from the government. The amount of alcohol you can purchase on a permit depends upon your salary. The higher the salary, the higher the amount of alcohol you're allocated. I would have thought that people with low salaries had a greater need to drink.

The UAE is truly a jewel in the Arabian Gulf. But you don't call it the Arabian Gulf in Iran. There, it is known as the Persian Gulf. So when you go to Iran, don't make the same mistake I did. (Americans can ignore this advice, of course, since Iran doesn't want you there anyway.)

But back to my story. As we gazed out over the ocean from our balcony, I stretched out my feet and took another sip of my wine. I held a smug smile, looked at my lady and raised my glass, "Here's to the tax men."

She smiled and reminded me that, in order for me to enjoy a tax-free income, I had to have an income first. I was in Abu Dhabi as an accompanying spouse and on her sponsorship. Yes, you have to be sponsored to live here, and since she was the breadwinner, I was at her mercy. Did it hurt my manly ego? Of course not—I was already halfway through the bottle of wine. I grabbed it again to refill my glass.

I've been told that red wine is good for you. I just can't remember if it's a glass a day or a bottle a day. I'm happy not knowing the answer.

2

WELCOME TO ARABIA

What is the first place you come to when you arrive in Arabia? Like in any other country, it is the immigration desk. And followed by immigration is customs. The first thing you will note at the immigration line-up, especially in the stricter countries like Saudi Arabia, is that time has no value. Tired after a long journey, you stand in a long queue that on a good day moves at a speed of about ten feet an hour. And under no circumstances should one attract the guards' attention or complain, as they are likely to send one to the end of the queue. Once you reach the immigration officer's desk you better have your landing card filled out right or otherwise, to the end of the queue again.

To further complicate life, there are five prayer breaks a day, and it is not at all surprising to find that when one is just about at the front of the queue, a prayer break is called. And that is it. Everything shuts down for twenty to thirty minutes and you wait while they pray. And remember, no complaining or it is off to the back of the queue again. I have spent anywhere from an hour to three hours getting through the immigration line. And you are only halfway through the process since there is customs to go through yet.

Customs in some of the Arabian countries is not what you are used to in the western world. To survive custom checks here first you need to be aware of dozens of unwritten local laws, but that won't be enough for you to survive the grueling ordeal. What you will really need is a sense of humor. Let me explain.

Once when coming into the international airport of Riyadh in Saudi Arabia, I brought some chocolate bars for my children. You know, the ones you buy from duty-free shops at the airports to fight your guilt because you forgot to buy something genuinely from the country you were in. My excuse was that I didn't have time to get away from meetings, while in all reality it was long hours at the bar and frivolous chitchat with business acquaintances that robbed me of time. Somehow it never seemed right to tell your business contact in the bar in the middle of a drinking party that you have to slip out to buy a Barbie for your daughter. So the size and weight of chocolate bars grow with the extent of one's guilt.

The customs officer, holding two large chocolate bars, one in each hand, glared at me and asked, "Alcohol?"

I realized that bringing alcohol into this country was like cutting your own throat and so I hurriedly responded, "Absolutely not. These are for kids…babies, very little babies. No alcohol in these chocolates. Absolutely not."

Needless to say he didn't believe me and unwrapped the corners of both chocolates, took big bites out of them and stood there chewing. Of course, one can't tell if there is any alcohol in chocolates by taking just one bite, even if it is a monster bite, so he attacked them again with his wide-open mouth and flashing teeth. Finally, he had eaten at least half of both chocolates. He nodded his approval, wrapped the remainders in their golden covers and put them back in my briefcase. Now you understand why only a sense of humor can help you in situations like this.

On a different occasion, a British gentleman ahead of me was being searched and questioned by a customs officer. In his small case they found a vibrator. Now life in Arabia can be dull at times, but bringing a vibrator through customs is like bringing a loaded gun through US customs. The officer raised it high in the air and demanded an answer as to what it was. With quick presence of mind, the British guy grabbed the vibrator and put it on his nose and said, "It's to wear on your nose like clowns do. It is for children's parties."

The officer tried it on his nose, gave it a look of uncertainty and finally let the British man pass. Well, sometimes you get lucky.

Don't even think of bringing videos, paintings or photographs into Saudi Arabia. I will never forget the day when a rather large American lady muttered inaudible curses under her breath while the customs officer kept tearing away pages from her magazines that contained either partial nudity, or uncovered shoulders, or advertisements for alcohol and so on and so forth. After removing about one third of her magazine pages he returned the magazines back to her, which she swiftly threw away in the garbage on her way out—not quite the welcome she was expecting.

Would you believe that there is a whole army of workers with black ink markers who every day go through every newspaper and magazine that comes into this region and black out all undesirable items? Yes, you guessed it: uncovered shoulders and alcohol advertising, as well as other offenses.

One of the scary things in Saudi Arabia is that when you come to work in this country they take your passport away. If you decide to leave on vacation or permanently you are required to acquire an exit visa first and when all formalities are cleared only then are you allowed to leave.

This may amuse you. Once they spent millions of dollars in an advertising campaign to encourage tourism in Saudi Arabia only to realize about a year later that there is no such thing as a tourist visa in that country. You can only visit Saudi Arabia on business and only when you are invited and sponsored by a local or a local company.

Drugs. You don't even want to think about bringing drugs into this part of the world. In Saudi Arabia they used to print in red ink on the landing cards: 'Dear visitor, we behead drug traffickers.' And yes, they do behead those who are caught with drugs. The justice system is swift and effective.

The authorities at the airport have the power to put you back on the plane you came on if you prove to be a nuisance. So if they eat your chocolates, tear away at your magazines, confiscate your videos, and destroy your books, consider yourself lucky and just stand there and smile. Otherwise, they may charge you for bringing contraband into their country and for that you could be punished by imprisonment, public lashings and finally deportation.

Welcome to Arabia.

3

THE TAX MAN COMETH

It is a known fact that two things are certain in life: death and taxes. Okay, so you have heard this one before. But wait. Now there is an exception. The best-kept secret of the modern era is—wait for it—the income tax-free region of Arabia. Yes, you heard me right. There is no income tax in the Gulf countries. Not only that, there is no tax of any kind in this part of the world, no GST, PST or HST (Americans would have to ask their Canadian friends what these abbreviations means). There is more. The GCC governments have devised labor laws under which all employers are obliged to pay for their employees' accommodations, transportation, annual return air fare to country of origin, an additional at least two weeks salary for every year of employment, and the school fee for their children, all free of charge. So what you earn is what you save.

In the past four decades, westerners increasingly have been coming to the

Arabian world to enjoy its tax-free environment. The odd thing is that even though patently obvious the expatriate community wouldn't admit that they are here for the money. I guess being greedy doesn't sound nice, does it? I don't care what people might tell you, everybody knows why they come to Arabia. Oh, I know people will tell you that they are here for the sunshine and adventure, but that is all hogwash. The primary reason is money. Greed.

Greed is good. It helps you live better. I don't know why people don't like this word. The English dictionary describes it as an 'overwhelming desire for more.' To me it sounds more like a definition of passion. I like passion, don't you? Look at it this way. We educate ourselves for years to carve out a career that will give us a comfortable lifestyle and the potential to save for retirement. Let's face it. Working in Canada isn't going to do that. Not for an average professional anyway (we can't all be hockey stars). No sir, not while Revenue Canada is in charge of the moneybag.

First you pay a hefty income tax on your gross salary and then you pay more taxes on the already taxed income in the form of Goods and Services Tax and

Provincial Sales Tax, harmonized or not (Canadians will understand exactly what I am talking about). Of course you are expected to pay unemployment insurance and other such deductions. You'll be lucky if you come out with one-third of your gross salary after all the taxes. And if you manage to invest some of your already heavily taxed income and by a fluke make some money, then the government will be there demanding taxes on that income too. You see, in countries like Canada there is a simple rule: You have money, you give a huge chunk of it to the government, you lose money, and the government doesn't know you.

So, one expects a little break from the government like writing off interest on mortgages against taxes. Most civilized nations' governments offer this. But oh no, not in Canada, here they take it away and then they take away more. So what do we do? We come to Arabia to enjoy a tax-free income. Be greedy, and why not?

So I decided to jump on the bandwagon and got myself a consulting job in Saudi Arabia to enjoy a six-digit income and zero tax bracket. Ah, that feels better. But the nightmare was just around the corner. You can imagine my horror when one sunny morning I saw in a Saudi local newspaper an announcement that, with immediate effect, all expatriates must pay income tax. This new rule was the result of a royal decree issued by the King's court. You don't get to question and deliberate on those.

A proposed 35% tax on gross salary (including all benefits) meant an income tax of about 70% on one's salary. Most expatriates immediately forgot the benefits of sunshine and adventure and threatened to resign unless the government agreed to reimburse the taxes. I guess that proves my point about the greed, but I won't press the issue. The government was not about to go against the wishes of their king and simply shrugged their shoulders. Would you believe that the international airline, in addition to their scheduled fleet, chartered planes to cope with the impending mass exodus of cash-flushed expatriates...proving greed rules again (sorry, I had agreed not to mention it again)? Actually the industry calls it economic opportunities. Whatever.

So, here we were, ready to pack up and come back home with our tail between our legs. We sat amongst friends and neighbors in the evenings and muttered that Canada wasn't so bad after all. At least our kids could play ice hockey (not a popular sport in Saudi

Arabia…actually, it is non-existent. Not much ice there.) And all the taxes we pay? Well, they are put to good use: education, social and medical services. It is a good thing. A good citizen should care about such things and contribute to building a better community. What a load of…but, anyway, we brainwashed ourselves enough to minimize the pain we were feeling.

A ray of hope shone when expatriates who worked for the airline (the only airline in the Kingdom) resigned and as a result the whole facility was grounded. Expatriates working in banks, oil and gas production facilities, and power generation facilities started to resign to go back to their home countries followed this. The princes (and there are about ten thousand of them) who primarily own most of the major local businesses realized that the country was on the brink of economic collapse and they made an urgent plea to their king to reconsider his new tax policy.

Within two days of the first announcement of this income tax a new decree postponing taxes was announced. That was good for the expatriate but not so good for the ruling family. To admit to such a mistake, well, is embarrassing. This may not be entirely true but rumor has it that the following Friday a couple of advisors to the royal court were beheaded. Talk about losing your head over giving bad advice. Ouch. Sorry, a bad joke.

Our greed-laced life returned to normal and I am happy to report that the Canadian expatriates are back to their favorite gossip— bashing Revenue Canada. The sunshine reports and adventure travel stories are in vogue again. That is until such time that the Kingdom again implements its tax policy. Remember, they have only postponed and not cancelled their policy on taxing expatriates.

Oh, I forgot to tell you that the Saudi government has been trying to bring taxes to expatriate income now for some fifty years. I guess the expatriates can map out long-term plans for adventure in sunny Arabia. Ah, eat your heart out H&R Block.

4

PLEASE SET YOUR WATCHES

A long time ago, in the faraway land of a magical kingdom, in the year 1433...wait just a minute, this is not a story of some distant past, it is now. That is right. Did you know that according to the regional or Hizri calendar (that follows the Islamic system), the current year is 1433? Trust me, this is something you really need to ponder in order to understand the gravity of the complications it entails and continues to generate.

It is intriguing, for the first 579 years (after the Gregorian calendar came into effect), when the Christians were using the Gregorian calendar to make their appointments for office meetings and what not, what were the followers of the Hizri calendar doing (since there wasn't any Hizri calendar then). I mean, how do you plan your week when you don't know what a week is? Okay, you say that is irrelevant—people in those days didn't have office meetings or need to plan their weeks. I could challenge you and ask how do you know, or why then the Christians needed a calendar? But never mind; let's not go there.

But answer me this. How did the Islamic people know how old they were or, more interestingly, how did they plan their vacations? Now, don't tell me they didn't have vacations in those days either. There I will challenge you because the one who must not be stared at has continuously told me that the concept of vacation started with the creation of mankind. Trust me, she knows, besides, she quotes facts about how even God had to take the seventh day as a rest period to enjoy some quality time with his family.

Consider this. I can't imagine any businesses of that time period surviving the accounting process. Mind you, some clever businessmen would have turned the lack of a calendar to their favor. For example, Enron would have loved to conduct business during the first 579 years in Islamic countries because they would have no requirement of filing financial statements, not at least until the Hizri calendar came into effect. Wow, 579 years of raping and pillaging shareholders. It sounds like every CEO's dream.

Actually, not having a calendar isn't all that bad. Can you imagine a world without tax accountants? If there were any then they would have had to wait for over 500 years to find a client. Sounds delicious. Here is another advantage that comes to mind. Gifts. One never had to buy gifts for anniversaries, birthdays or any other annual occasion. I bet that the married couples then lived happily because there was no way one could be angry at a spouse for forgetting their wedding anniversary birthdays. So, there you have it. You not only saved a fortune on gifts but you also never had to figure out if it was your paper or diamond anniversary.

In those days I imagine one had to choose a life partner based on how one looked, not knowing how old the person was. Not like today when macho men like their brides to be young and firm. It sounds like one is acquiring fresh fruit or checking out an expiration date before making a purchase.

Sorry, I digress. But I am sure not knowing how old a person was must have had its own unique problems. How could any government know when to make you a pensioner or bars knew if you were of legal drinking age. I am sure you young people reading this story are now rubbing your hands together and wishing you had lived in those days so you could go to any bar and drink as much as you liked. Okay, so these weren't the most pressing issues in those days or certainly not in the Islamic countries, but you must admit it's mind-boggling.

I believe that the Islamic scholars were either confused at the time or wanted to differentiate their people from the rest of the crowd, because when they finally started their calendar system, they made Saturday the first day of the week. Their weekend is Thursday and Friday and this hasn't changed in the Kingdom since the inception of the Hizri calendar.

It causes a lot of confusion, to say the least. I still remember when, as a new expatriate in Saudi Arabia, I reported for work on what I thought was my first day of employment and my employer reprimanded me for not turning up for work for two days—not a good way to start a new job. It takes the expatriate community forever to get used to the Hizri week. Somehow after living for decades under the Gregorian calendar it is difficult to go to work on Saturday and Sunday. Funny though, it took the expatriate community no time at all getting used to not going to work on Thursday and Friday of every week.

Life is really sweet if you are working for a western firm in the Arabian Gulf for you will find that effectively you work only three days a week—Saturday and Sunday being holidays in the western world and Thursday and Friday being holidays in the Arabian Gulf. I don't think too many western expatriates will appreciate me putting this in the press, but there you are.

I do believe that the Islamic scholars of earlier times were looking to differentiate themselves because Hizri is a lunar rather than a solar calendar. Now, this has a certain complexity. It makes all the major Islamic festivals fall on different dates every year. It may add differentiation but I sure am glad that they didn't take this concept too far and made the start of their working day at moonrise. Can you imagine working through the nights and sleeping through the days? Boy, it sure would have made the electric companies rich.

One of the funniest stories I have ever heard in Arabia, and this may not be true in its entirety (but anything here seldom is), is that some time ago when a British Airways passenger plane was approaching the Riyadh International Airport, the captain on the PA system announced, "Ladies and gentlemen, thank you for flying British Airways. Let me be the first one to welcome you to Saudi Arabia. We are on our final approach to the Riyadh International airport, please make sure your seatbelt is fastened snuggly and if you like, you may adjust your watches to the local time. Please put it back by 580 years...."

I was further told that British Airways had to pay a hefty fine and the captain in question had to submit a written apology to the local authorities before he was allowed to take off. English humor is misunderstood in most of the world, don't you agree?

Now if you will excuse me, I promised my kids I'd take them to TGIW because it is a Wednesday night. Get it?

5

HELLO, HELLO, HELLO

Let me ask you this. When your boss enters your office first thing in the morning, what do you say to him? '*Good morning.*' Right. And five minutes later when he comes back because he forgot to tell you something, what do you say then? *Nothing.* Right again. You just give him an inquisitive look and wait for him to speak to you. Right? Wrong. Well, I am sorry to tell you this but you won't do very well in Arabia. When your boss in Arabia comes into your office, this is how the conversation goes (translated into English for the benefit of those who can't understand Arabic):

The boss will say: "Hello."

You'll reply as you stand up: "Welcome."

Then the boss says: "Peace be upon you."

You'll respond: "On you be peace."

Then: "Good morning."

And you will say: "Good morning."

So far so good, but we are not quite done yet. By now your boss most likely wearing a big grin will shake your hand by slapping hard his hand into the palm of your hand. Be careful with this manuevor as doing wrongly it could break your thumb. He would then say: "How are you?"

Of course, your answer would be: "Fine, thank you. And how are you?"

"Fine with the grace of God," he would reply.

"What is your color?" would be his next inquiry.

"Excellent with the grace of God," will be your response now.

If you find this to be a little tedious then here is the clincher. Every time, and it doesn't matter if it is ten times a day, this is the first conversation you will always have with your boss when he enters into your office or you his office. You heard me right, every time. Give me that 'howdy partner' any day—it allows you extra time to drink more coffee.

Now here is something I won't ever forget. Once I walked into an Arab gentleman's office and his phone rang. Yes, you guessed it; he had to go through the ritual of saying hello and asking for health in a variety of ways for about five minutes before he said—*sorry, wrong number*.

Arab hospitality is legendary. Last weekend we went out camping in the desert with our Arab friends. I was impressed when observing that every time a SUV would come near our campsite, its Arab owner would stop and walk up to our campsite where our friends would offer him tea and chat with him in a warm and friendly manner like he hadn't seen him for months. What is a SUV? Where have you been for the past two decades? SUV is a gas guzzling, small house on four wheels that has become a preferred mode of transportation for the modern world. Besides, in Arabia you need it to participate in demolition derby motorsport that they play everyday during rush hours. Where was I? Oh yeah, so my frinds shook hand, kissed on both cheeks and hugged and spoke in excited voices with the guest. With an inquisitive look I said, "Wow, it is amazing that so many of your friends are also camping in this area. You must be a popular man?"

My friend shook his head and with an expressionless face responded, "These aren't my friends. They are strangers lost in the desert inquiring about directions."

You see what I mean. Everything here seems like a ritual. What is good that they have time for both friends and strangers. They are never in a hurry. That is except when they are behind the wheel of a car during rush hours. Then their schizophrenic side takes instantaneous hold of their otherwise congenial personality and turns them into something of a road demon. The speed at which you can travel by car is only limited by your vehicle's capability. The highways are built here to support my theory. They are almost straight without many bends or curves, eight lanes divided, floodlit and without highway patrol cruisers with speed guns—whether they are a highway to heaven or hell depends upon if you hit something or not.

Mercedes Benz, the flagship of the German auto industry, prides itself in making safe cars by using a steel body cage for extra protection. Once in Saudi Arabia I saw a Mercedes split into two halves that were lying about fifteen yards apart. The impact must have been so severe that it had spliced the steel body cage into two neat halves. I am not going to tell you what lay all over the road between the two halves but as my emergency physician wife says, it's always good for business.

Doing one hundred miles an hour in a car is common. I am talking about driving on the city roads. On highways when I am driving one hundred miles an hour I could be the slowest driver, and cars will pass me at a speed that I hazard to guess would be around one hundred and forty or so miles an hour. Now picture this if you can. Peripheral vision blocked by headdress, rearview mirror purposely adjusted to look at and admire your face, mobile phone pressed against one ear, your other hand now and then fiddling with the car CD player or assisting you to sip on hot Starbucks or picking your dried up nose, and your car flying at one hundred and forty miles an hour on a straight highway to….

And do you know why they drive as if there is no tomorrow? Because they believe their life and death are in the hands of their God. If God wants them dead then they will be dead. No question. What they don't know is that their God was a wanderer of the desert and never had the experience of driving fast cars. If he did then I am sure He would have devised a new sermon that would have said something like—*don't be in a hurry to get to me, drive slowly*.

Last weekend driving back from Dubai to Abu Dhabi, I was clocking one hundred and twenty-five miles an hour and enjoying myself. My wife gave me a stern look as if to say—*don't be an idiot, slow down*. I misread, purposely, her expression and registered it as—*you're my hero...fly me to the moon*. I didn't see the police car in the slow lane doing one hundred miles an hour. I lost concentration for a fraction of a second and swerved a little too close to the police car and almost hit it. That was not good. Flashing lights and a siren pulled me over. There was no mistake in reading the expression on my wife's face this time, she was wearing a broad grin and looked very satisfied with the outcome. She waited for the fun to unfold.

In my side mirror I saw the angry face of a menacing looking policeman. I rolled my window down and now I could hear abuses and curses coming from the policeman approaching my open window. He was slightly frothing at the corner of his mouth as he adjusted his sidearm. I stepped out and to my utter amazement the policeman extended his arm and said, "Peace be upon you." Automatically I responded, "On you be peace," and so on and so forth. There never was a question of a ticket or warning, just an exchange of nice words with a hint of dissatisfaction that my car was swerving. I love Arabia and its hospitable manners. It gives a new meaning to road rage. Vroom, vroom....

6

THE ART OF GETTING A DRIVER'S LICENSE

I have sat through several exams during my high school and university studies and like the majority of students I dreaded them all. They aren't fun, are they? They cause undue stress and increased tension that I am sure is not good for one's health. I think every exam sheet should carry a surgeon's health warning just like the one we see on cigarette cartons. But none such exams ever gave me as much anxiety as when I had to take a driver's license test in Arabia.

Now, I do have a long history of taking these tests. No, I didn't fail it several times, how dare you? It is just that I have moved a lot in my profession and had to take a driver's license test in every country where I became a resident.

It all started a long time ago in India when my father in his 1947 Ford Mercury drove me to a neighboring town about thirty-five miles away where we entered a regional driver's test center for my driver's test. After my father had a word with the examiner, he came and sat in the front passenger seat next to me and asked me to drive away. Now that posed a minor problem. I had never driven a car in my life before. I had only watched my father drive and that was about four times a year. I looked in horror at the examiner and said, "I don't know how to drive."

"Then why are you here?"

I looked pleadingly out of the window and at my father who was standing under a tree and he nodded his head and smiled. I nervously started the car and proceeded to engage the first gear. The examiner quickly interrupted my progress and said, "That's enough. Come inside and get your license."

As he stepped outside the car I noticed a big grin on his face and a hundred-rupee note sticking out of his shirt's top pocket.

Years later, and I should mention that after I had taken several driving lessons, I took my British driver's license test in England. I will never forget the conversation I had with the examiner after I finished the test. He had asked, "Are you planning to drive taxi cabs? It is just that you are okay as a driver, but will need more practice if cab driving is going to be your profession."

"I am working on a Ph.D.," I answered, casually wondering if he knew what I meant.

"Well, that is good if it helps you improve your driving. Taxi driving is a responsible job. I know all you Indians and Pakistanis come here to drive taxis and buses to support your family and I admire this in you people. So that your family faces no hardship, I am going to pass you, but remember to practice."

How could you argue with such a kind man? I thanked him and promised him I'd look into a taxi-driving career soon after I had completed my Ph.D.

A few years later I took a driver's test in Canada. I made a mistake of immigrating to Canada in winter and they told me it was one of the worst winters they had seen for decades, -55 degrees. I see you ask Fahrenheit or Celsius. Doesn't matter, it was bloody cold, okay? Now just imagine for a moment. There I was in a silk suit, Italian pump shoes, driving a monster-size car with steering on the wrong side and taking my driver's test on a day when black ice on the road and ice crystals in the air would have proved a daunting challenge even to the likes of Michael Shoemacker and Emerson Fitapaldi. I can just see their faces with sheepish grins as they read this article. Mind you, I passed the test, but I don't know how because my body was frozen and my mind was numb. I was just grateful and to be honest amazed that my car started in -55 degrees Celsius temperature.

But none of this had prepared me for what lay ahead in the Kingdom of Saudi Arabia. My employer told me that my Canadian and British driver licenses were no good in the Kingdom and I must go to the appropriate authorities to get a Saudi driver's license. I even tried my Indian driver's license and for a moment I thought they were going to accept that as a requisite to issue me a Saudi license. But alas, no such luck. So, I took myself to a place on the outskirts of the city where driver licenses were issued. After I paid a few hundred Saudi riyals I was given a blue folder that included an application form and instructions on how to fill out the form, all in Arabic. But not to worry, I was told to go outside the building where under the shade of a lonely tree I would find some Sudanese and Egyptians who for a few riyals would fill out my application. I was told to use the Sudanese. But that is another story and it will just have to wait.

And they did fill out my application that included not only my name but my father and mother's names and their parents' names, my religion and my blood type, any previous conviction, what I was doing there and when was I going to leave their country. I took my duly filled-out application and lined up with the rest of humanity to wait for my turn in a long queue. When I reached the front I noticed a small window about fourteen inches wide and twelve inches high and behind the window was a human voice that demanded my application and a few more riyals. As I slipped cash and my application through the tiny window, someone behind the window grabbed my hand and pulled it in. Next thing I noticed or rather felt was that my arm up to my elbow was yanked in and a sharp needle was piercing my skin. The voice said, "Blood. You must give blood. It is compulsory. Don't move your arm."

I was rigid with fear as they drained my blood. Next the voice asked me to read a chart for my eye test. I tried to look through the tiny window for the chart but there were none to be found. It was rather dark inside the room. A rather large gentleman with a frizzy Afro hairstyle from Eritrea standing behind me poked his thick fingers in my ribs and gestured that there was a chart behind the man who was sitting behind the window.

I tried again but couldn't see the man behind the window, let alone the chart behind him.

I stuttered a few words of frustration and that seemed to annoy the gentleman behind me more than the man behind the window. He said something incomprehensible that I am sure was equivalent to adjectives such as imbecile or stupid or Christian and he shoved a piece of paper in my hand that was a copy of the eye chart.

I quickly read the first two lines and at that point the voice behind the window shouted, "Good. Next?"

As I retreated from the window I wished my father were still alive because I am sure he would have found a way to slip the man behind the window a few hundred riyals to get me a driver's license. Cooperation through corruption, yep, it would have worked.

7

BEWARE OF THE ROAD SURPRISES

Back in Canada I paid attention to road signs because they were put there for the safety of motorists. Here in Arabia I believe they were placed for the amusement of motorists. I say that because some of the road signs on the Arabian highways are baffling to say the least, but always amusing.

Driving to Dubai from Abu Dhabi, about an hour and a half journey if you are an expatriate living here or thirty-five minutes if you are a national, you will notice a huge, blue sign that reads—Beware of Road Surprises. Now what the heck do they mean by surprises? You look around curiously but apart from nationals passing you at breakneck speeds of over one hundred and twenty miles an hour, you don't see too many surprises. Maybe they are warning us of camels that sometimes drift onto highways and look at those fast moving box-like objects, wondering where everybody is going in such a hurry. Or could they mean those nationals whom you sometimes find occupying two lanes by driving at a snail's pace side-by-side with their windows rolled down, having a chat. Oh yeah, they could drive slower if they wanted to.

Actually, surprises on Arabian highways can come in a variety of forms. You may find a few cars parked on a hard shoulder and not necessarily behind each other, huddled and blocking the slow lane because a few local friends have decided to stop and have a picnic by the roadside. Picnicking by the roadside is a popular thing here. On the other hand it could be speed bumps some construction firm overnight put into the middle of the highway in an effort to slow down the motorist for no apparent reason. You should see the black marks that rubber tires leave behind as motorists try to reduce their speed from one hundred and twenty miles an hour to zero miles an hour in five seconds. Yes, people here don't just slow down to go over the road bumps, they actually come to a full stop, look around to see if anyone can explain why they are there and then ever so slowly they allow their cars to climb over, and then back to Formula One spirit as they increase their speed to one hundred and twenty miles an hour.

Bumps are known as humps here, and a typical road sign will say—*Hump ahead for one hundred meters*. Now in my country humping is a private thing and to do so in public takes a lot of guts. What takes even more guts is to hump for the whole one hundred meters. Only a select few can do it.

Then there are road signs that are just precious. You may come to a road junction and the road signs will tell you, no right turn, no left turn, and definitely no entry straight ahead. Now what you do is at your own peril. One of my wife's favorite signs at the mouth of a narrow street read—*No entry except for prayertime*. So, what happens when you ass an Arab enter into this narrow street at prayertime and see a monster truck driven by a Christian driver coming head on? Well, the answer is obvious: you pray. Then there is a sign at a T-junction that reads one-way street to the right and one-way street to the left and two-way streets both ways. I have a theory that authorities who are pro-road rage are deliberately putting up these signs for nationals to vent their anger so there will be no time for them to think about other issues like restrictions on the dress code, strict laws about alcohol consumption, and rules that forbid kissing in public.

Oh, I forgot the best part of the 'Hump Ahead' signs. They look like two breasts without the nipples. Mind you, some artists have been at work and now they look much more appropriate.

There are no shortages of road signs in fast-developing Arabian cities where you are advised to either turn right or left except there are no roads to turn into. This has its advantages. It allows you to practice emergency braking. I remember being advised by a helpful soul, when I asked him about a certain destination, he had said, "Go straight down for about twenty miles to the end of the highway and then at the T-junction, it is all sign posted, you can't miss it." Simple enough. When I reached the T-junction I did find a pole mounted with two empty frames in the shape of arrows pointing left and right but there were no signs inserted yet. Needless to say I used common sense and flipped a coin.

I love the signs at the hospitals, such as no sounding of horn. Once a national who had parked next to such a sign honked to get my attention and asked me what that sign meant? He was just being friendly and inquisitive. Locals definitely disobey one-way street signs and their excuse is that they are only going a short distance. Well, everything is good in moderation.

Then we have my absolute favorite: roundabouts or traffic circles. In the UK, motorists in the roundabout have the right of way, while in Europe the motorists approaching the roundabout have the right of way. Can you imagine how confusing this could be in a region like Arabia where so many nationalities coexist? Back in North America we are clever and have very few roundabouts or maybe it has to do with our lack of ability to think while we drive and do other things like chew gum, sip coffee, answer our cell phones, and flip the bird. You get the drift.

As the story goes, in Riyadh, the bustling city of four million people in Saudi Arabia, a survey was conducted where Britons, Europeans and the nationals were asked about the right of way in a roundabout. As you may suspect, the Britons said that the guy in the roundabout has the right of way and, of course, the European disagreed and insisted that the car approaching the roundabout has the right of way. The interesting answer came from the nationals who vehemently insisted that they had the right of way because it is their country. Now don't laugh because there is a lot of truth in it for that is the way they treat their roundabouts. If you have any sense, you'd better let the nationals drive the way they want and always give them the right of way.

It wasn't so long ago when, if in an auto accident with a national in Saudi Arabia, it was always considered your fault because you were there. You see their logic is that if you weren't in their country in the first place the accident wouldn't have happened. I can understand that, it is their country and they make rules that suit them best. One morning I was awakened by the police, taken to a station, charged with negligent driving and fined for the damage to a national's car as well as mine. As I looked at the officer inquisitively with bewilderment written all over my face, he explained that while I was asleep the national crashed his car into my car that was parked outside my house. And yes, you guessed it. The policeman reasoned in a serious voice that such an accident could have been avoided if I had not come to work in their country.

There is no specific point to be made here except that if you do intend to venture into driving in some of the cities here, make sure you bring one hell of a sense of humor and a lot of cash to pay fines. Happy motoring.

8

DEVELOPING THE SIXTH SENSE

They say that in the Middle East one needs to develop a sixth sense, especially when one tries to drive a car in the busy cities of Arabia. The concept of traffic lights is rather new to the region. It was not so long ago when the locals here freely roamed their towns on the backs of their camels. To make a leap from that to driving in fast cars, trying to stay inside marked lanes and stop just because there are some colored lights on a tall pole is rather a tall order.

It is not so much the size of the car as it is the owner of the car that decides who can be the big bully on the city's busy streets. The rich families here are considered invincible and to follow traffic rules, like the masses try to do, is rather beneath them, or at least it seems that way when you see them driving, as going straight through red lights is their prerogative. And this, especially after you have developed the sixth sense, makes the hair on the back of your neck stand up as you approach red traffic lights, for you can sense the danger around you.

The other day I read an article in the local newspaper on police who, to demonstrate how people fail to stop at the red lights, had set up a surveillance camera at a traffic light and caught 150 offenders in just four hours. That is more than half the drivers who went through that traffic light in said period. Then there are the U-turns. I haven't seen them in too many countries but they are really popular here. At almost all the traffic lights, one is allowed to make a complete U-turn. You should see the smoke and noise that comes from the squealing tires as motorist make U-turns on busy streets at about fifty miles an hour.

To see a motorist driving by occupying two lanes at the same time is not an uncommon sight. Some of the drivers believe that the white line on the road is something you straddle with the center of your car to maintain a straight line. Sounds logical, doesn't it?

It is in this country that I found the definition of a Nano second. It is the time a car behind you takes in hooting its horn the instant the traffic lights go from red to green. The traffic lights here take a long time to change. The reason is that at a traffic junction it is only one set of traffic lights at a time turning green. People always carry a book or newspaper in their car and read when the lights are red. Another observation you will make when waiting for the traffic lights to change from red to green is that cars start to gather all around you in what looks like a rugby scrum. And when the lights change to green there is honking and maneuvering to get ahead of the guy in front.

For a person in the far right lane to cut across all three lanes to make a left turn at a traffic light is quite common and this is where the sixth sense comes into play. When you are ready to take off from a traffic light you must plot your strategy to dodge the cars coming at you from every direction. One easy solution is that as soon as the light turns green, you close your eyes and put your foot down and test the car's acceleration, to take you from naught to sixty miles an hour in four seconds. This may pose other problems, but it sure will get you ahead of the pack in the rugby scrum.

Now if you were to assume that there are no penalties for traffic violations in Arabian cities, then you are in for a shock.

Most traffic violations go unnoticed because the traffic laws are poorly implemented but I can guarantee you this, once you are caught and charged with a traffic violation, you are going to remember the penalty for the rest of your sane life. Here is why. For example, in the city of Riyadh, the penalty for the first time offender with a minor traffic rule infraction, say lack of use of indicator or inappropriate change of lane, you may receive a several hundred-dollar fine or several days' imprisonment. For a similar offence, the second time will attract both fine and imprisonment. The third time not only you will lose the use of your vehicle for several days, but you will also be whipped in public every day of your several days' imprisonment.

Now for a serious offence like jumping the red light, the automatic penalty includes several hundred dollars in fines, several days in prison and whipping in public every day of your imprisonment for every male member present in the car. Only children and women are exempted. Yeah, you heard me right. You don't have to be a driver to be penalized. Being in the car at the time is enough for you to receive the same treatment as the offender. Did I hear you say it is not fair? Well, you can appeal the charges, not that it will do you any good, and it could automatically double your penalty if you lose the appeal.

Oh yes, one more thing. Until recently it was considered illegal to have auto insurance. You see it interferes with the will of God. If God wanted you to kill someone and then be punished, insurance companies must not interfere with the will of God. Once again, the penalties for injuring or killing someone in an auto accident are pre-established. For example, if you kill a local, you would pay what they call blood money. Trust me when I tell you that it's a dandy agreement because it wasn't that long ago when the eldest son of the deceased was given the right to cither choose the blood money or to put you in the middle of the road and run you over. Yes I see you agreeing, so don't complain just pay the blood money.

The payment schedule for the blood money was also pre-established. For men, about $40,000 for an Arab national, $30,000 for a non-national Arab, $20,000 for a non-Arab Muslim, and about $8,000 for a non-Muslim. If you thought that's unfair, try the penalty schedule in case it's the death of a woman. It was typically half for women compared to men with one exception. For killing a Christian woman in a road accident, there was no charge. Now I haven't looked into the penalties for some time and may be a little off on the amounts, but you get my point. So you see, the sixth sense is something you develop when you live and drive in this part of the world.

Then there is a religious month of fasting. During this month the Muslims are not permitted to eat or drink from sunrise until sunset every day. Driving takes a whole new meaning during the religious month of fasting. Somehow aggression multiplies several-fold when you haven't had anything to eat the whole day and are driving back to your home at sunset to put that first morsel in your mouth. Your best bet is to stay off the road at the hour of sunset. If you can't do that then watch out for those fast-moving, swerving cars and get out of their way for they won't stop at any red light at traffic junctions. It is chow time and no little red light is going to stop a hungry man from getting to his meal.

If you must drive in this part of the world, please be sure you drive a big truck. A Hummer if you can buy one would be perfect. Get rid of the horn and have your Hummer fitted with machine guns. Oh, and make sure that your life policies are up-to-date and your will and last testament are current.

Happy motoring. Got to go now, I hear my taxi waiting outside.

9

BLOODY SUMMER

The ultimate dictum in my life is: 'From the frying pan into the fire.'

Now, if you promise not to whisper a word of it to the one who could kill you with a frown and melt you with a smile, then I will share with you the mystery behind the above cliché.

As a boy I grew up in the central part of India in a partially renovated old (we're talking maybe several hundred years old) house with no air conditioning. To get air, you went outside. The summer temperatures would reach in excess of 100 degrees Fahrenheit and in no time envelop your body in prickly heat. And this was when we were still inside the house. Outside, the dust-laden, hot air will whip up the temperatures even higher and severely diminish your life expectancy if you were to work or play outdoors. A typical morning greeting in that part of India wasn't good morning or hello, it always was: 'Another bloody hot day.'

Now, one has to be a hell of a good salesperson to sell living in the Middle East to a person with such a miserable experience of growing up in a hot and dusty environment.

But then I never said that my lady was an ordinary person. As you can see, despite my adverse reaction to heat and dust, here I am away from the cool of the Canadian Rockies and living in the Middle East. It suits her best because she grew up in Saskatchewan where winters are long and temperatures could drop to minus 60 degrees Fahrenheit.

Now imagine this if you can. The summer in Abu Dhabi lasts for about nine months with at least four months of intense heat, where day temperatures soar to 120 degrees Fahrenheit and night temperatures aren't much better, around 95 degrees Fahrenheit. If that wasn't enough to cook one's goose, the humidly is over eighty percent. I am not exaggerating when I tell you that here I have seen flies in summer lying spread eagle on their back on the sidewalks gasping for air. I'm not kidding, you can dress up in a sleeveless T-shirt, shorts and beach sandals and go out for a walk after dark and you won't last but only two to three minutes before you find yourself drenched with sweat and the rubber soles of your sandals melting on the hot sidewalk.

When I first moved to Arabia (did I mention I moved there in summer?) from Calgary, my body had to go through a drastic change to adjust from minus 60 Fahrenheit to 120 Fahrenheit and so did my wardrobe. In Calgary you are accustomed to putting on layers of clothes before you head out, but in Arabia you start peeling layers off as you go outdoors. The real challenge in summer is to bring home from a supermarket a tub of ice cream without it melting. We tried everything, from buying it as a last item and then driving to home at 100 miles an hour (not stopping at the red lights, of course, but then nobody did), to using a cooler as a transport container, but nothing was really effective. Yet it was a challenge, you see. Every time we would buy an ice cream tub and make a mad dash to the house, and my little boy would give a running commentary, "It is okay…now it is melting in one corner…now it is very wobbly…it is pink, Dad…it is on my legs now…there is a mess on the car seat…pink looks good on blue fabric…can I lick it, Dad?"

We tried many times and ended up spending a whole bunch of money on several tubs of ice cream but alas, my children had to grow up without having the luxury of eating ice cream by the pool.

There were other incidents to remind me of the perils of an Arabian summer. Once when I was in a romantic mood (it has been known to happen just about every year), I bought an audiocassette of my wife's favorite music. Before leaving for work, I placed it on the dash of her car to surprise her. When I got home she was furious. She asked me if I had left an audiocassette on top of her car's dashboard. I admitted sheepishly that I did buy her a surprise gift, knowing full well that I had made a mistake, but didn't know where and what. I was about to be enlightened. She took me out and showed me the plastic top of her dashboard where the audiocassette had melted under the heat of direct sun and fused into the material of the dashboard. It was now a permanent fixture on the dash as the molecular bonding was too strong to scrape off. I think the title of the music cassette was: 'Summer Love".

See what I mean? I can't imagine anything too romantic about a burning sun. Mind you, my children always enjoyed cooking eggs on hot stones outdoors. And you know what, they will eat them too. If you were to prepare them a healthy breakfast in a clean frying pan and ask them to eat it, do you think they would pay attention? No, but they would scrape messy egg off the dirty, hot outside stones and eat it as if it were a delicacy. Don't start me on children or I could go on forever.

When you think about it, certain aspects of the below-freezing temperatures of Calgary and burning-hot temperatures of Arabia are the same, just opposite in nature. Confused? Let me enlighten you. You still have to wear gloves to touch the burning hot metal under the Arabian sun. You must also wear gloves in the freezing Calgary weather. Also, you need to start the engine and turn your air-conditioning on full blast for fifteen minutes before you can get in the car and drive off. Much like having to start the heater in the car before driving in extreme cold. Only here I have noticed that people have dual air-conditioning units in their cars: one in the front and another in the back.

Here is another problem of a slightly different kind. No air-conditioning system in the world is perfect. In office buildings where they pump chilled air through large air-conditioning machines, the chiller is forced to work extremely hard, i.e. at full capacity to cope with the excessive heat beating down on the large glass windows. Arabian summer is the only time I know when you have to wear a sweater to cope with the freezing temperatures of office buildings inside. Now, instead of coffee, this is a place where they should store and serve ice cream. Just a fleeting thought.

Here is a bit of information I have been told is true. The governments of all Arabian countries have made a law that people don't have to do any outdoor work if the temperatures are at or above fifty degrees Centigrade (122 degrees Fahrenheit). Great, you might think, but it doesn't really work. Why? Simple, because of officially and according to the Ministry of Meteorology the temperatures tend to get stuck at 120 degrees Fahrenheit. I bet you my first born that if the Arabian governments increased the limit to, say, 125 degrees Fahrenheit, the reported temperatures will then reach at least 124 but never 125 degrees Fahrenheit. Get it?

Oops, here comes my lady! I'd better wish her a good morning (because I can only inwardly say—*another bloody hot, sunny day*), start her car to cool it down, put a sweater in her car, get her gloves so she won't burn her hand on the car door handle, make sure nothing is placed on her car's dashboard, and put some chilled water bottles in a cooler in her car—what a marvelous start to the summer, and I cringe to think that it will last for the next nine months.

I envy Eskimos.

10

HOW TO BE ON TV

When I first arrived in Arabia I never had to use the phrase: 'Pass the remote please.' Let me explain. So often I hear from my friends in North America that the television has taken over their lives. Now that one can have the choice of hundreds of channels, one can spend his/her entire life learning new things and have no time to ever make use of them. Parents are having a tough time getting their kids to do outdoor activities but do not take blame for giving them their own TV sets on their fifth birthdays. And to make matters worse, kids don't even have to get up to change channels for all TVs come with remotes.

Here we have a slightly different problem. During the time of the Gulf War, I was working in Saudi Arabia and noticed that they had only two TV channels: Saudi Arabia One and Saudi Arabia Two. Actually, there was only one channel because Saudi Arabia One was in an Arabic language and the same content was broadcast in English on the Saudi Arabia Two channel. Would you believe it if I told you that I used to surf between the two channels just to beat the boredom of having only one channel?

My favorite program was the nine o'clock news. It always started with the reading of telegrams that the King had received from the dignitaries of various countries that day. It took about five to eight minutes to read those telegrams. Then came the interesting part. The next five to eight minutes were about the telegrams that the King sent to various dignitaries in response to the telegrams he had received. And would you believe I sat in front of that TV set every night at nine o'clock listening to all those telegrams.

The rest of the news was about the King attending various local functions or receiving certain dignitaries who were visiting the Kingdom. Such news typically showed a large room with highly ornate furniture filled with various ministers dressed in similar traditional regalia sitting around bleary-eyed due to the strong TV camera lights. Rarely would they have news about neighboring countries, the international content of the news.

You may ask: *why didn't the people have a TV dish to overcome this shortage of programs?* Well, the importation of a TV dish was legal and one could buy such a thing in the open market but its use was prohibited. And if you did manage to get a dish installed then you ran the risk of the religious police taking a pot shot at your dish and punching holes in it, rendering it useless.

Well, the Gulf War changed all that. The residents of Saudi Arabia were following the news of the Gulf War on their transistor radios (I don't expect you kids in America to understand what a transistor radio is, ask your grandpa) and were unhappy because they couldn't see the video images of the scuds and patriot missiles fireworks on the TV. The Arab channel did not admit that the nation was at war (they were waiting for the royal decree to make the announcement) and continued to read the incoming and outgoing telegrams. Mind you, there was a marked decrease in overseas dignitaries visiting the King that should have given the nationals a clue.

On the fourth day of the war, and especially when thirty to forty scuds a day started flying into Riyadh from Iraq, the national TV admitted that the country was experiencing a kind of conflict with a neighbor. Okay, if you prefer, at war. Religious police were asked to take a holiday and the TV coverage was relaxed. Then CNN roared in and provided the Rambo-style, blow-by-blow coverage of the Gulf War.

My favorite war program was a daily summary report telecast in the late evening. There would be a panel of four generals of the allied forces including an American, British, French and a local to give accounts of their sorties carried out that day over Iraq.

The American general would have an interactive slide show with video footage showing exactly what their smart bombs accomplished that day. They bragged about how they were winning this war on their terms and the Iraqi army was no match for their technologically superior armaments.

The British with their single flipchart drew a few circles with bright red markers and explained their tactical maneuverings of the day while stiffening even more their already stiff upper lip. They affirmed every evening that Her Majesty's forces were making jolly good progress and were quite capable of defending the Raj. Say what? The French general never bothered to get out of his chair and always leaning back, looking relaxed, would mutter something like they could be better but were concerned about the discomfort the French legion was facing because of the unavailability of alcohol (and women, though he didn't say it too loudly). The French general always hinted that their weaponery was just as good if not better than the Americans (in the hope I'm sure that in future Iraquis would buy French weapons).

Of course the best was the local general. He would replay all the slides and videos of the Americans, make use of the British flipchart and totally ignore the French general. The presentation of accounts given by generals of respective daily sorties was always followed by a question and answer session. While the American, British and French generals always attempted to answer the questions that were specifically directed at them, the local general always delegated his answers to the American and British generals, obviously ignoring the French general again. Obviously it does not pay to criticize one's country while you are there.

Most work here is contracted to foreign companies and expatriate workers carry it out. To fight a war was nothing more than yet another contract that was given to the allied forces to fulfill. It is wonderful to be rich, isn't it? As patriot missiles fired by foreign soldiers knocked scuds out every night from the Arabian skies, a popular saying emerged— *only two things are needed to fight a war in Arabia: patriots and expatriates.*

Although the Arabian television allowed the foreign channels to come into their region, the programs were heavily censored. Watching an edited foreign program on TV was like playing a game known as, 'Fill in the blanks.' The news was only as good as your imagination. And then arrived the wonderful programs that could be broadcast unedited on the local TV, like the history of the Canadian Rockies. You may not appreciate it, but sitting in the sweltering heat of 120 degrees Fahrenheit watching the snow-clad mountains of the Canadian Rockies was (to borrow a phrase from my son) 'cool.' It also made the locals happy because their camels looked much bigger than ours (moose).

I always wanted to be on TV and just realized how I could be on the national television here. I am going to send a telegram to the King of Saudi Arabia.

11

LAWRENCE OF ARABIA

We have all heard of the fascinating history of Arabia. My curiosity started after seeing the movie *Lawrence of Arabia*. Wipe that smirk off your face, we all have to start somewhere. Anyway, I was informed that there is an entire ministry in the Kingdom of Saudi Arabia that caters to information-hungry people like me. I was delighted to learn this and one fine morning I drove to the ministry of information. My four-year-old son accompanied me on the trip to ministry, as the one who must never be argued with informed me when I was getting into the car that she had a bridge morning and the maid was sick. Well, I thought this could be a fine opportunity for me to spend some quality time with my son.

We chose a couple of his toys to take along, a bright orange plastic gun and a rubber snake. My son knows how much I hate snakes but he insisted on bringing it because he claimed that seeing his father frightened made him forget about going to the toilet. Well, whatever works, I thought. I didn't want to look for toilets on my way to the ministry so Mr. Snake came too and sat most of the time on my steering wheel. Those of you who don't have kids yet won't understand the humor in it but just you wait…we the married are all doomed and there are no two ways about it.

Where was I? Oh yes. So off we went to the ministry and arrived at the gate at about ten in the morning. At the front gate of the ministry building I found myself face-to-face with an armed guard. I wondered for a minute if I should just sneak through the gate or if I should wait for the guard to give me some signal that I could go through. You see I didn't want him to shoot me in the back. That would have made it difficult for me to get my son back to the house before my lady wife returned from her bridge game. I held my son's hand tightly and approached the guard to say politely (in my broken Arabic), "Excuse me, sir. Can I go inside to get some information on Saudi Arabia?"

From the grimace on the guard's face and his firm grip on the rifle at his side it soon became evident to me that the guards from the National Security Forces of Saudi

Arabia were trained to strictly follow procedure, nothing more and nothing less.

The guard gave me a stern look and demanded, "Letter?"

"What letter?" I whimpered.

"A letter issued by the ministry authorizing you to enter this building. No letter, no entry."

"Okay," I said nervously. For a moment I thought of calling it quits but then I saw the expression on my son's angelic face that said—*Plug him, Dad*.

I mustered up my courage and decided to stand my ground and asked, "And where do I get this authorization letter from?"

"Inside the building," came back a short but firm reply.

I wondered if the guard was joking. Could he have a sense of humor? That would be a first. But the soldier appeared to be serious.

"Wait a minute," I tried to reason with him. "I can't go inside the building without the authorization letter and the authorization letters are available only inside the building. Is that correct?" I found his logic, or rather the lack of it, to be more amusing than frustrating.

"That's correct." He was discharging his duty as told. Good soldiers don't ask questions, while better soldiers don't even think.

I knew then that there was no way I could go inside the ministry of information. I looked at my son and shrugged my shoulders. We were about to leave when a Saudi man came out of the building and approached me. He spoke in perfect English, "Is there something I can help you with?"

"This guard tells me that an authorization letter—"

I didn't get a chance to finish my sentence as the man burst into laughter. "I know the routine. You cannot go inside and the authorization letters are inside. You think you've got a problem. I work here and some days even I cannot go inside the building."

He took my passport details and asked me to wait while he went back inside and about half an hour later reappeared with an authorization letter for us. The Saudi told me that next time I must file an application by fax to request an authorization letter and once I received such a letter only then should I come to visit the ministry.

The guard took my letter and held it upside down in front of his face, pretending to read it, and told us to go right ahead. I am sure the guard did not know how to read but he had recognized the royal seal on the authorization letter, which was enough for him to permit us to enter.

Once inside I was told to wait because only the director of the facility could give out the information. I didn't argue because there was another armed guard in the lobby who was staring at me with fierce eyes. He had an even bigger rifle. I waited while my son wandered about in the lobby. About five minutes later the guard came towards me and he was holding my son's hand. He told me my son was cute but I should not leave him unattended.

My son has this uncanny ability to disappear right in front of my eyes. I don't know how he does it but one minute I was watching him playing with his toys and the next minute he was gone. I looked at him and what I saw horrified me. My son was holding the guard's rifle and pretending to shoot him with it. The guard pulled something out of his big belt and pretended to shoot him back. It was my son's bright-orange, plastic gun. They were, of course, playing cowboys.

I waited for about two hours while the soldier thoroughly entertained my son, or maybe it was the other way around. I was assured that I would see the director before he left for lunch and told to be patient as he was busy. I didn't see anybody else waiting there, so who was he busy with? Well, I didn't feel like going through some cumbersome process of applying for an authorization letter for the next visit, so I waited.

At one o'clock I was advised that the director had to rush out and now wouldn't be able to see me today. Perhaps I would like to make an appointment for the next week. I didn't believe the clerk because I didn't think the director was capable of rushing anything or I would have been seen by now.

I don't have to tell you that I never went back to the ministry because I was certain the next time I would take my son there with a real rifle. I do still enjoy replays of *Lawrence of Arabia.*

12

DESTINATION RESORT

Here is a novel concept. Having used oil wealth to modernize the country and build an incredible infrastructure, the government of the Kingdom of Saudi Arabia embarked upon promoting their country for tourism. It is a multi-billion dollar industry worldwide and they didn't want to miss out on such a great opportunity.

Well, it isn't quite that novel an idea because neighboring countries like United Arab Emirates, Bahrain, Oman, Qatar and even Yemen have opened up their doors to tourism and a great many numbers of Europeans now regularly come to these countries to escape their harsh and long winters. Besides, the images of *Lawrence of Arabia* and *A Thousand and One Arabian Nights* conjure up such romantic ideas in the hearts of the young and adventurous that the thought of roaming around in the dunes of the Saudi desert gives them the feeling of being a modern Lawrence of Arabia.

But tourism in Saudi is a bit of a novel idea. Why? Because in Saudi Arabia one cannot get a tourist visa—there aren't any, provided you are not counting going to pilgrimage a tourist activity? This may be a minor detail to some but one must be able to get inside a country first to fully enjoy its culture and color. So, why did they decide to develop tourism when no one can enter the country? The answer could be as simple as there are two different ministries involved and they often don't consult with each other prior to developing their plans. Sounds incredulous? It gets better.

A while back I read in the local press that a tourist company did manage to book a large group of tourists from European countries under some kind of a trade visa and brought them to Jeddah, the famous port city of Saudi Arabia on the Red Sea. Upon their arrival, tourists were told to take a day to rest in their five-star hotel while the arrangements for the rest of the week were being finalized. The company had promised the Arabian adventure of a lifetime. The group didn't see much need of a rest after only a six-hour, direct flight and were dismayed to find that no alcoholic drinks were permitted in the Kingdom. After drinking copious amounts of tea and non-alcoholic beer, they retired for the night.

Early the next morning they gathered in the lobby, men in their bwana, khaki safari suits and ladies in long, cotton dresses (to make sure no parts of their bodies were visible, a local tradition and requirement). The tour operator apologized for the strict dress code and presented his defense that too much exposure in the hot, Arabian sun could be harmful. Most tourists whose almost transparent-looking white skin made them resemble albinos shook their heads in disapproval. After breakfast they were told that the permit to visit the city was held up and lunch would be served early in case anybody was hungry. Some of the members of the group were still having their coffee and finishing their breakfast.

Late afternoon arrived and still no city permit. The tour company apologized once again and at about five p.m. threw a lavish barbecue for everyone. It was slow cooking on lukewarm charcoals. It improves the flavor, explained the tour operator, who was smart enough to keep at least an arm's length from the big guys.

Another day of rest and everyone retired early. The morning of the third day came with same uncertainties and the entire day passed without any tours. Needless to say, an early lunch and later on a slow barbecue dinner were provided by the tour operator.

On the fourth morning there was ominous feeling in the air. Having spent half their vacation in a hotel lobby, the group's mood changed from frustration to anger, as they demanded their money back and a flight home. The tour operator maintained his distance from his clients and explained that it could not be done. He apologized, saying, "I'm sorry, but to get you out of here we must apply for an exit visa."

"So, do it," growled a three-hundred-pound Bavarian man.

The wheels were set in motion and all passports were submitted to the ministry to obtain exit visas. By now you must have gathered that in Saudi you need an entry visa and once there you will need an exit visa with a few exceptions, where one can obtain an entry and exit visa simultaneously (rather rare) or a multiple entry visa (extremely rare).

Late on the fourth day, the tour operator at the barbecue explained that all was not lost. Ministry, while processing exit visas, had granted permission for some events and tomorrow the group could expect wonderful treats. Although dejected from their treatment thus far, some of the members of the group felt that at least they could take some snapshots to prove to their friends back home that they had been to the mysterious Kingdom.

Day five and everyone were dressed up to head out. They had loaded their cameras and stuffed extra film in their backpacks. The tour operator explained that cameras must be left behind, as photography in the Kingdom is a dangerous thing. One is not allowed to take pictures of people and any object of military and national importance. And guess what? Every building, bridge, road and so on was considered of military importance. Tourists reluctantly brought their cameras back to their rooms and waited in the lobby for the tour bus. An hour later the word came that the ministry that gave permission for a city tour didn't have the authority to do so and a new application to acquire a permit would have to be filed with the appropriate ministry.

Day six and at breakfast time the tour operator rushed into the restaurant to announce to the group that a great slide show of wonderful sites of the Kingdom had been approved by the ministry and such a slideshow was to be organized in the evening in the comfort of the five-star hotel. After the barbecue dinner everybody was invited to this magnificent slideshow absolutely free. The tour operator ducked just in time to protect himself from flying grilled tomato missiles.

Tourist visas are still strictly forbidden in the Kingdom.

13

LAW & ORDER

The Arabian countries are very proud of their law and order. And they should be because the crime rate here is very low. They proudly claim that in their major cities the crime rate is significantly lower when compared with the major cities of the USA. Very few serious crimes like murders and rapes take place in Arabian cities. The key to their success is swift and harsh punishment.

The burden of proof is more on a defendant than on prosecution. It is almost as if everyone is considered guilty until proven innocent. In some of the stricter Islamic countries there are no fancy courts, jury systems, proper defense representation and an appeal system. Once arrested you are likely to be sentenced in a very short period of time, no long deliberations and complex legal technicalities. Crime cases are judged, typically on Fridays, the day of a big religious sermon by the head of a mosque and he and he alone can pass judgment based on laws of their holy book.

A friend of mine once gave me invaluable advice: never commit a crime on Thursday in Arabia since Fridays are judgment days. For any serious crime such as murder, rape, child molestation and dealing in drugs the automatic punishment is death by beheading. They take you out to a public square, labeled chop-chop square by expatriates, where blindfolded, you are forced to kneel down. As an executioner's buddy jabs a small knife in the lower back of the convict for his body and head, to provoke the reflex to sharp, sudden and intense pain, jerking back, the executioner brings his sword down in an arc like swinging of a number one wood, and takes off the head. If he ever loses his job as an executioner, I bet he could give golfing lessons.

Well, it doesn't work every time and sometimes it may take three or four tries, just like my tee shot with a driver, before the head is severed from the body. My sensitive wife is horror-struck by this and pointed out to me that it must be very painful when they jab that pointy knife in the lower back of the poor prisoner. All my assurances to her that it doesn't really matter because before he can ever feel pain, his head is taken off haven't consoled her troubled mind.

So remember never to try your luck with a serious crime in this part of the world or certainly not on a Thursday or you may have only one night to live. Can you believe that some of the countries in Arabia used to telecast beheadings as prime time entertainment? The legal system here makes no distinction between locals and expatriates when it comes to punishment. Don't expect your embassy to defend and protect you, they are not here for you, they are here for one thing and that is making money from oil trade.

When a murder is committed in a small Arabian village the legal system allows the police to arrest the whole village and throw them in prison indefinitely and until such time that the villagers decide to reveal the name of the man or woman who committed the crime. God help you if the villagers don't like you.

This may amuse you: As an expatriate and because you are unfamiliar with local customs, you are allowed a local defense attorney but only after you have been charged and convicted. So what can a local defense attorney do? Well, obviously not a lot but the authorities are ironing out some of the wrinkles in the system and hope to improve upon it in the next forty to fifty years.

Now women generally don't get beheaded for their serious crimes. No, no, they are the more delicate race and, rest assured, are treated with humanity. A woman convicted of a serious crime is forced to kneel in a public square and then the authorities bring an eighteen-ton truck loaded with large, sharp and heavy boulders and they empty the truck on her. Stoning by throwing small pieces of stones one at a time takes too much time in this busy e-commerce society.

Minor crime brings severe punishment too. For example, if you steal or shoplift or pickpocket, then as just punishment you are likely to lose a hand by amputation. Unlike in the old days when they hacked your hand off by a sword, in the current modern era the punishment is carried out on a much more humane basis—they surgically cut off the offending hand. After a long and hard battle by various international humanitarian organizations such as Amnesty International, the laws here have been altered. Well, just a bit. One is allowed to appeal to the religious court against his or her charges but there is a caveat. If one loses the appeal then automatically the previously established punishment is doubled, both hands are amputated. You guessed right, there are hardly any appeals in this part of the world.

As you can imagine, the crime rate is very low and I am all for swift punishment. What is the point of spending millions of taxpayers' hard-earned dollars on criminals who in all likelihood are not going to contribute much to society anyway? Weed them out, I say. One has to set an example and that is a no-nonsense system of quick and sharp justice with harsh punishments.

During prayer times when every shopkeeper takes off to the neighborhood mosque to pray, they leave behind unattended and unsecured shops that might have millions of dollars worth of goods on display. Does it tempt people to shoplift or steal? Absolutely not, and you know why? It is because anyone would find it difficult to enjoy life with both hands missing. If you accidentally drop your wallet filled with cash and credit cards in the middle of a street or at a shop, then what are you supposed to do? Go to the police? No, no need. Go back and retrace your path and the wallet will still be lying exactly where you dropped it.

When you arrive in this part of the world your embassy would advise you that most of the countries here are not countries, they are kingdoms and sheikhdoms. That means they don't recognize any international laws and international laws have no jurisdiction here. It is like entering into a big family and one had better obey the family law. At best embassies can observe but cannot intervene into local law and order proceedings.

Whenever I tell these stories to my friends they sit with slackened jaws and give me an inquisitive look that says—*so why are you still there? Isn't it too dangerous?* And my answer with a sheepish smile is—*there are worse things in life. For example: the taxman. It is all a matter of choice, a slow agonizing life made hellish by taxes or a tax-free glorious life that comes with quick death in case you murder someone.*

I know what I choose.

14

LEBANESE BARBER

In the Arabian world it seems that certain jobs are monopolized by certain nationalities. For example, most waitresses are Filipinos, most taxi drivers are Pakistanis, and most barbers are Lebanese.

I am rather particular about where I go for a haircut. No, don't get me wrong, I am not a fuss pot, it is just that I have only a few hairs on my head and I'd rather they stay there for a little while longer. So when my hair started to crawl down my collar and began to cover my ears, I thought I could sport a Phil Collins-style hairdo or maybe I was on my way to a Willie Nelson haircut. But then 'the one who must be obeyed' started to roll her eyes every time we went out on a windy day when my hair resembled that of Don King, and I had no choice but to find a barber. I decided that it was a safe bet to go to an expensive salon in a five-star hotel and so I chose the most costly one in town.

A Lebanese who spoke Arabic with a French accent greeted me and pointed towards a sink. I took my glasses off, folded and then then put them in my shirt pocket. I slipped into a small leather chair for my hair to be washed. That was painless. After washing my hair, the barber sat me down in a large, red-leather chair and assuming a contemplative mood he asked, "What do you want done with your hair?"

Now I had already researched this by talking to several friends who were experienced in this kind of thing to know what one must *not* say that could be otherwise detrimental to the outcome of one's haircut. For example, don't say—*I don't want it cut short*, because the only word they will register will be *short* and you know what you are going to get: a short haircut. So I squinted but all I could see was a blur in the mirror and nervously but cautiously responded, "I want to keep it long, just tidy it up."

That should do it, or so I thought. Most discomforting, though, was that I was the only customer at the time, there were three barbers (I presumed they were barbers, otherwise what were they doing there?) in the shop, and they talked constantly, watching soccer on TV and drinking espressos, all at the same time...and one of them was trying to give me a haircut. As the clicking of scissors sounded in my ears I said politely, "I like my hair parted high-up in the middle and not way down on the side."

His immediate response was, "I will cut it in such a way that you can part it anyway you like."

Now how could you argue with that? I resigned myself to the fact that there was nothing more I could say or do since he was the one holding a sharp instrument in his hands. After a few minutes he turned his attention to me and said, "I noticed with your booking that you are a doctor. Where do you work?"

"I am not a medical doctor," I replied, hoping this wouldn't disappoint him and hurriedly added, "I have a doctorate degree in engineering."

"So are you a good doctor? I have this problem," he continued as if he never heard me. He took out a sheet of paper from a drawer and shoved it onto my lap, muttering, "My cholesterol is too high. I don't have time for exercise and love Lebanese food. What shall I do, doctor?"

Now I knew I was being trapped. If I refused to give him medical advice (which I was not qualified to do, as I am not a medical doctor), he was bound to give me a short haircut. I smiled and squinted at his reflection in the mirror and said, "It seems that your triglycerides are high and high density lipids are too low. Your low-density lipids are high and that is not good. You must get your triglycerides and low-density lipids low and high-density lipids high. If you are not good with diet and exercise, then why don't you go on medication and start with 20 mg. of Lipitor?"

Impressed that I knew this stuff and horrified that I was dishing out unqualified medical advice? I thought you might be. Well, I know it because his lipid profile looked similar to mine and I effectively told him what I was told by my doctor. The unqualified advice I had to give because I love my hair and would do anything to protect it.

You should have been there to see the instant recognition I got from all three barbers. More medical reports in my lap and a fresh cup of espresso and some dates with almonds in them. There was a new enthusiasm in my barber's agile fingers as his scissors clicked away with a new ferocity. Shorn of hair, as bits and pieces were flying, dropping all around me, all I could do was sit there wrapped in a white apron that was too tight around my throat, squinting and armless. Every time I tried to free one of my arms from under the apron so I could touch my head to feel if there was any hair left, my barber's body immediately blocked its movement and he continued to dance around me like a matador.

Finally he put his weapon down, removed the apron and fixed his gaze on my reflection in the mirror. I could only guess that he had a quizzical look on his face demanding my approval. I squinted hard and nodded slowly. I reached for my glasses, put them on and looked at the stranger in the mirror. My hair was so short that previously thinning areas were now bald patches. My hair was parted so low on the right side that it almost touched my right ear. As I looked at the barber in bewilderment, he flashed a big smile and snapped his fingers as if to say there is more to come. I took out a hundred-dirham note (about $30) in disgust and threw it across the counter, promising myself never to return to this high cholesterol joint.

He looked at the hundred-dirham note and seemed eager to show his appreciation for such a large tip. The tip was for me to escape from him with whatever was left on my head and not for him to do anything more. He misunderstood. With the heel of his left hand on my forehead, he forced my head back and with some pointed, sharp scissors he started to snip my nostril hair. My entire body and mind froze in horror. With my eyes tightly shut, I prayed it would be over soon. Suddenly his scissors were clicking in my ear and now my ears were being made hairless. Then it stopped. I kept my eyes shut and slowly lifted my arms to touch my nose and ears. That was a mistake. Suddenly he forced my right arm up, pulled up my shirtsleeve and with a buzzing sound shaved my right armpit. The same treatment was repeated for the left armpit.

When and where it would stop, I wondered. With my hair on my head, nose, ears and armpits gone, a terrifying thought flashed through my mind. With lightning speed and my hands covering my crotch, I bolted out of the barber's chair and ran for the exit.

15

CAMPING IN THE DESERT

When the Safestway (that is Safeway Arabian-style) invited us for their annual camping event in the desert of Saudi Arabia, we were delighted for two reasons— *adventure and payback*. Well, we believed that since over the entire year we had paid so much money to the store for drinks that looked like Coca Cola, breakfast cereal that pretended to be Kellogg's, and Belgium waffles that were made in Yemen, you know what I mean—*premium prices for off-brand products, it was payback time*.

My wife, two kids and I jumped in our SUV and joined a hundred-plus group of various shapes and sizes of SUVs in the supermarket parking lot and headed out to the desert camp. The convoy was led by a group of five Toyota pickup trucks driven by Filipinos who worked at the supermarket. They were heading in a general southwesterly direction without any firm idea of where exactly the camp was. This became evident as we got lost three times and finally, instead of at noon, we arrived at the camp at five in the afternoon. Well, there was still time to enjoy a tranquil desert sunset before the lavish Arabian dinner promised, including a big BBQ (they have to be large to cook camels).

There were at least five hundred people present, and that put a dent in the tranquility we were so eagerly anticipating. I guess everybody believed in payback. As the sun started to go down, the wind picked up. The hot desert wind, called *Shamal*, that originates from the Sahara desert of northern Africa and sweeps through the great desert of Saudi Arabia before hitting various tiny Sheikhdoms on the Arabian Gulf and, in this case, our picnic, hit us hard. The wind was gusting at forty knots and one could feel the fine, hot sand hitting one's face like a million tiny pieces of glass, a great way to get your face sandblasted—*exfoliation, the natural way*.

The kids were hungry and now, being sandblasted, they were really cranky. The master and controller of our destiny spoke just two words—*home now*. Might I add that it was her idea in the first place to go out to a desert picnic, and therefore I wanted to say— *I told you so?* But I am not that stupid, I know that God has blessed her with a higher-decibels voice than me and she knows it. So I kept my trap shut and looked at her with that blank expression on my face that I am so famous for.

Well, needless to say we neither saw the sunset nor did we stay for the feast. We bundled the family back up in our SUV and headed home slowly, finding our way through yellow fog. You see I am not very fond of sand. It gets into your eyes, crunches in your mouth between your teeth, plugs your ears, blackens your nostrils and finds itself into unmentionable places. You can't see, can't breathe, can't eat and can't enjoy the sunset, so I ask you—*what on earth does my wife see in going picnicking or camping in the desert?*

To me sand is associated with beaches, and beaches are associated with the ocean and the ocean is where you find palm trees, warm breezes and blue water. Ah…and add a margarita to that. This is what dreams are made of. A desert is nothing but burning hot winds, millions of tons of sand without any water for fun and frolicking, and no palm trees for shade. And forget about that margarita in the Saudi desert unless you are hankering for a lashing followed by deportation.

Recently when my wife's niece arrived from Canada, we (well, not quite we, it was the wife) decided to take her out on an overnight desert camping trip. While we sat on top of a sand dune gazing at a million stars and getting sloshed on homemade wine, a *Shamal* kicked in. The wind started to whip our faces and we started to drink more to fight back. The more we drank, the fiercer the sandstorm became, or at least it felt that way. Our hair became rigid coated with fine sand it stood on end like antennas and when I started to feel that sand was ramming its way up between the nails and flesh of my big toes, I realized that we were beaten by the power of the sandstorm and must retreat to the safety of our tents. Nature can be so vindictive.

Tents? They vanished, sailed off on stiff winds, nowhere to be found. Drifting aimlessly in a blinding storm and shouting for our tents to come back at once, we realized that we were hopelessly drunk and in no shape to fight the might of millions of tons of sand flying around, mainly in our faces and under our big toenails. All three of us huddled in our SUV and waited out the storm that finally subsided at seven in the morning. Groggy, hungry, with newly sandblasted red faces and sand-coated afro hairstyles, we made our way back home and ended up giving quite a fright to our maid, who set our dog on us.

My wife and the idea of desert camping seem to be engaged in a constant duel. She keeps trying and still has not learned her lesson, even after losing expensive cameras, several contact lenses, tents, and mobile phones to the romantic notion of overnight camping in the desert. For an engineer like me, it is quite simple. Nature, like any other wild thing, needs taming and is best observed from a controlled environment like an air-conditioned enclosure. Nature is like a woman. The more you think you understand it, the more it springs surprises on you and they are rarely pleasant. But you are brainwashed to take pleasure in it. Like claiming in an exhilarated voice—*what a wonderful desert camping trip it was*—knowing full well that all your experience included was the loss of valuables and suffering from hunger and lack of sleep.

Wait a second. I think I just heard my wife shouting for me, I've got to run. I forgot we were taking her ninety-year-old mother visiting us from Canada to an overnight desert camping trip and must pack snorkels as protection for contact lenses against sandstorms. Catch you later.

16

DUNE BASHING

A wise man once said that if God wanted us to fly He would have given us wings. Well, it didn't stop us from designing the flying machine and despite all the crashes, hijackings, terrorist attacks and other problems inherent in that practice, we continue to fly and ignore the wise man's advice.

I wonder why men have a suicidal streak in devising things that can injure and kill. Okay, I can understand flying because we can get to from place to place in a short period of time. But activities like climbing Mount Everest where the chances of dying are higher than the chances of making it to the top, now where is the logic in that? Even the great Sir Edmond Hilary, when asked why he climbed the mountain, answered—*because it is there*. Now people of a philosophical nature hailed that as a great answer, but it is quite obvious to a rational person that he didn't really have a good reason. Can you imagine for a moment a bank robber telling a judge that he did it because the bank was there and he hoped to get away with it? Not likely. He might be sent first for psychological evaluation, but eventually he would be thrown in the slammer. You got off easy, Sir Hilary.

Dune bashing could easily fall into the same category as climbing Everest. Now most land vehicles are designed for driving on blacktop roads. Some road enthusiasts were not satisfied with that so along came the SUV to take them off-road. People here, locals and expatriates alike, enjoy going to the desert in their SUVs, camping, picnicking or simply for joy rides. Those that are man enough, or would like to be considered as such, take their SUVs to climb tall and steep sand dunes and then slide down, at the risk of tipping the vehicle over. They call it a rush, which rational people know as being synonymous with stupidity. Anyway, that is what we call in Arabia dune bashing.

Last week my wife made an allegation that, according to her, we don't do enough to spice up our lives. No, she wasn't thinking a week in Tahiti. It was a request for us to go on a dune-bashing trip. Now, most of the time I let her have her way, but there are limits. When she showed me a little advertisement in a local magazine of a company that organizes dune-bashing trips (I didn't know till then that there was such organized foolhardiness), the only thing that caught my eye was the first line—*we train all our guides in first aid*. You tell me, does that sound like a great promotion for an exciting time?

Most travel companies try to attract your attention and get your business by offering free champagne on arrival or one free night in a hotel or free breakfast, but never free first aid service. I decided to be civil about it and planned to offer her logical answers as to why we should not deliberately do something that could leave us paralyzed for the rest of our lives. And if that didn't work, I decided to put my foot down and flat-out refuse.

Thursday morning, the start of our weekend, we were in our SUV following the dune-bashing guide, heading for the Liwa sands where dunes are exceptionally high. Once we reached the edge of the sand dunes, we were advised to lower the tire pressure from 30 psig to 15 psig to get better traction (I'm sure it didn't do any good to those tires), engage four-wheel drive, shift to a lower gear and say a prayer or two. With my heart in my throat and hands gripping the steering wheel so hard that my knuckles turned white, I ploughed my SUV into ascending and then descending dunes.

The SUV wobbled dangerously, threatening to flip over or turn on its side, while my wife shrieked with joy as if she was a cowgirl riding a horse in a rodeo. And if that wasn't enough, she slipped an Enigma CD into the CD player, turned the volume up to the maximum, and rolled down all the windows. For a moment I had a glimpse of what heaven must be like when you are approaching it. I could almost see the white light.

Emotionally drained and physically exhausted when we stopped at the base of a tall sand dune, we waited for some of the other SUVs that were bringing up the rear slowly simply because they didn't have Enigma to boost their morale or to numb their senses enough to catch up with us and our guide. Two of the SUVs came off the dune and slowly drove toward us. One parked right next to us and another went slightly on an incline at the foot of the dune to park next to his buddy. And right in front of our eyes we saw the SUV on the incline slowly turn on its side and land upside down right on top of the SUV that was parked next to us. I guess the incline at a slow speed turned out to be more dangerous than bashing round at a high speed.

We all rushed over to get the passengers out of the upside-down SUV and the first-aid training of our guide became really useful. My wife was so happy that the guide was so professional and I was so mad because this is the type of madness I had been so ineffectively trying to warn her about. Needless to say we needed more than just the first aid, we needed a crane to rescue the two SUVs, and the remainder of the trip was cancelled without reimbursement. Thank God for that, I would have happily paid for the cancellation of this adventuresome journey before it started anyway.

On our journey back I saw an SUV perched precariously on the ridge of a tall sand dune and its owner hanging from the front bumper and swinging from it trying to dislodge it. Did he care, if the vehicle came dislodged, where it was going to land? No, no, of course not. Because to do such a sport he must have been soft in the head, don't you think? A one-ton vehicle landing on him would have simply killed him and put him out of his misery, the poor puppy.

The other day one of our friends came for dinner and over a bottle of wine described their wonderful trip to the sand dunes. They told of nature's stark beauty, brilliant red sands continuously drifting in strong winds, the wonderful sunset, and what an exhilarating experience they had. My wife gave me a disapproving look as she stared at them with envy and admiration. All I could hear was that they went out for a six-hour trip in the blistering sun and blowing sand and spent about four of those hours digging their SUV out of the soft sand. Do you think I am different from the masses here that seem to consider such miserable times as fun? I can live vicariously and enjoy every pleasure offered by sand dunes by watching *Lawrence of Arabia*, can't you?

People like my friends desperately want to be the modern day Lawrence of Arabia and are willing to pay any price for it. If I were one of them I would definitely take an intensive course in first aid or make sure that one of them is an emergency physician. Me, I get enough adventure roaring around in a golf cart on green rolling hills looking for my ball, which has a habit of disappearing in bushes and trees…I personally hate sand bunkers, regardless of their size.

17

A BEAUTY CONTEST LIKE NONE OTHER

Why is it never the woman's fault? The other day, my lady came home from one of her dreadful night shifts that finish at two in the morning and went straight into our kitchen to get some comfort food before going to bed. She was irritated to see a plate and spoon in the sink. Her irritation was due to being tired from working a night shift, but in her mind she believed she was irritated at me, because she had to come back to an untidy kitchen.

Now, did she notice that the whole kitchen was immaculately cleaned, the floor wiped, the kitchen counters scrubbed, and the dishes washed and put away in the cupboards? Well, if she did it didn't matter, because what she noticed most was that one last plate and a spoon in the sink. I woke up to loud banging noises in the kitchen. How could anyone make so much noise with one plate and one spoon?

And why did she have to clean them up at two in the morning? Well, I don't really know. If I did, then I'd bottle the knowledge and sell it to millions of frustrated husbands who are so desperately looking for answers.

Sorry, I digress. So, she'd already awakened me with her banging, and now she gave me a gentle nudge to make sure I was fully awake. She wanted to have a chat. A chat—at two in the morning! "Why don't you clean up after yourself? Well, I'll tell you why. It's because you are bored. You stay at home, always writing those '*1001 Arabian Nightmares*' stories. You're not going out enough. You should get out more. You need more fresh air, exercise and a good night sleep."

I was touched by her concern, but all I could mutter was, "I'm sleepy. Can we try to get some sleep now—at least a few hours in before dawn?" As I drifted back to sleep, I heard some muttering about being lazy.

In the morning her reorganization of my life continued. "We're going out today. We have to start attending social functions of some sort. I've arranged with some friends to go to a beauty contest. So get ready, we will be leaving in thirty minutes," she boomed. Her assertive voice is inversely proportional to her delicately built and petite body, which gives some a false impression of meekness. But I know better, oh yes, I do. I know when she says something she means it.

I was wondering, though, how an Islamic country where women are mostly veiled had permitted a beauty contest. I shrugged. Hey, I am all for reform, especially when it comes in the shape of all those half-naked girls swinging their hips…some might call it progress. I call it entertainment. I put on my best slacks and a silk shirt and expensive-looking dress shoes. My wife gave me one of those loaded looks, but I hadn't yet figured out which message it conveyed: *'fool', 'hopeless', or just simply 'men'*.

All my friends, whose own attire was quite casual, smiled at my clothing. I said nothing. As far as I was concerned, it was their loss if they didn't want to look their best. I wouldn't allow myself to be presented to Miss Beauty of the Year without appearing suave.

After about a forty-minute drive, we arrived at a large, open, desert area dotted with colorful tents. I gaped at a big banner that read—*First Camel Beauty Contest*. Everyone knew but me, no wonder they'd smirked at my clothes. I felt like a real jerk, wandering among the Bedouins and casually attired expatriates in my expensive silk shirt and dress shoes.

This contest was created to demonstrate the respect and love the people of the Arabian Gulf have for the camel, and the contest purse reflected that—*the first prize was one hundred thousand dirhams (almost $30,000).*

The contest had four categories: adults, individuals, those under two years old, and everybody's favorite, the camel studs. I can understand the first three categories, but how could the judges determine the winner for the fourth category without prying into the animals' private lives? And what would the judges demand as proof of their stud quality, camcorder footage? Well, I didn't bother to inquire for somehow it didn't seem appropriate with ladies present.

Mind you, the winning camel stud had huge eyelashes. He could have qualified for a new category of pretty boys. But that is only my opinion. I'm sure the judges knew what they were doing.

The following weekend, when my lady and her friends invited me to join them at another beauty contest, I was prepared this time not to be caught unawares. I dressed in casual attire: frayed denim cutoff shorts, sleeveless gym shirt emblazoned with the slogan *Touch, Don't Squeeze*, desert sandals, and a baseball cap. I was cool as a cucumber. I knew by now that this wasn't going to be a typical beauty contest. I'd be rubbing shoulders with camels. I knew there would never be pretty, half-naked women parading in swim gear anywhere in Arabia—at least, not in my lifetime.

It was an Arabian horse beauty contest. Some of the horses were worth millions of dollars, and so was the total prize money. And you should have seen some of those sheikhs and sheikhas—arriving in their Rolls Royce, Ferrari, and huge Mercedes—all wearing the finest European clothes and covered in a dazzling display of gold and diamonds. Needless to say, as the ladies of my group walked through the front gate, the security guards told me that the service entrance was at the back.

Yes, I again felt like a real jerk.

So when you visit Arabia and attend the local beauty contests, just remember one simple rule: camels mean casual and horses mean, well, one helluva lot. I know there is a lot of money in horses and they look magnificent when trotting or galloping, or whatever fancy words they have for their gaits. But one thing I'm sure of, that stud camel with the long lashes and the diamond tiara on his head is breaking the hearts of some young lady camels.

My wife is due home from that dreadful night shift again, and there's again a plate and a spoon in the sink, waiting to be washed. I'm going to go now to do wash up as I don't want her to wake me up at two-thirty in the morning again to tell me that we should go to the upcoming goat beauty contest. Once you've seen one, you've seen…well, you know what I mean.

18

WHICH WAY IS EAST?

Street names are rather a new and a novel concept in the major cities of Arabia. It was not so long ago that many cities had, and even now there are a few which have, no street names. When you gave someone directions to your house, you always drew a map showing major landmarks on the way to your house such as power pylons, a dead camel, kebab house, and a car wreck. Sometimes showing as your map landmarks objects like pylons could be confusing because they are forever constructing new residential developments and adding these pylons overnight, but a dead camel or a car wreck are a pretty safe bet.

Once I was invited to a dinner party and, of course, a hand-drawn map came with the invitation. Once I reached somewhere close to where I was supposed to be going, I got terribly lost and started to go in circles. My wife insisted that I seek help from the locals who were bound to know this area. I spotted four nationals in their traditional attire hanging out on the corner of a junction where four roads met and I knew I had been there a few times in the past twenty minutes. I stopped, got out of my car and showed them the map. All four heads buried themselves in the map and they turned it around in all directions to figure it out. You can ask any national here for help in finding places and they will never turn you down. They have oodles of time when it comes to helping a stranger, especially when that stranger happens to be with a blue-eyed, blond lady.

Finally one guy pointed straight on while the second pointed to the right. The third vigorously shook his index finger in the left direction while the fourth, wait for it, insisted I should turn around and go back the way I came and find some nice restaurant for my wife. They all vehemently defended their choice of direction and insisted that they knew the area well. I stepped back into my car, gave a big smile to my wife and followed the advice of the fourth man—*I went back and took my wife out for a nice dinner.*

Kids are very perceptive. They know immediately when something is wrong. Every time I took my two kids out for a drive more often than I care to remember I got lost on my way back home. Oh, no, nothing serious, eventually I always found the dead camel or that car wreck, but these landmarks have begun to appear in too many localities. A dead camel is a dead camel, right? My son would be the one who would whisper (loud enough so I could hear it) to his big sister that Dad was lost, *again*. They would stretch out on the back seat and catch a snooze while I frantically examined dead camels by the roadside to see which one was mine.

But it's not just me. Even the local driver I hired to drive my family around while I was at work would get lost. And he had lived here for the past fifteen years and had the advantage of knowing how to speak Arabic. Well, his getting lost adds an entirely new meaning to the term sense of direction, or rather the lack of it. When my wife would call him to come and pick her up from the Marriott hotel where she often went for brunch with her friends, he would set off to visit all the five major hotels in the city and eventually would find her.

When my wife complained that the driver took hours before picking her up, I confronted Hussein and asked him why. He shrugged his shoulders and said he got lost. But he was lying, it wasn't true, as I discovered later. His problem was that he was almost deaf and he would rather go to all the hotels in the hopes of finding my wife there than to admit that he was hard of hearing. He was also shy and felt very nervous about asking me to repeat myself. Maybe he was both deaf and shy. Since my wife went to different hotels to brunch, he obviously thought his system was effective, as he would always find her—*eventually*.

Well, one day someone at the city-planning department decided that they were going to name all the streets in the city of Riyadh. And it did happen but it turned out to be of little use. First of all, the signs were in Arabic and then, of course, all streets were given the name of the king and his family. So they all sounded similar and they were about ten feet long...royal family names here are rather long because they include almost all the names of important people in your previous generations—and they were all important.

The new roads that were not yet being considered by the city planner for naming were given names by the contractors who built them. Some of the contractors saw this as an opportunity and named the streets after their company's name—*free advertising*. Other contractors who were not so enterprising didn't know what to do and named each street according to its width. It is true. The Twentieth Street in Riyadh, for example, is not before Twenty-first Street or after Nineteenth Street, but it is twenty meters wide.

In Abu Dhabi, the logic behind naming streets is something of a mystery. If you travel down the Sheikh Zayed First Street for a while it then becomes the Sheikh Zayed Second Street and further down the road it is called Electra Street, while before it was called the Hamdan Street. They would have given this street a few more names but Abu Dhabi is an island and the street ran out of land. But no sweat, because I can guarantee you that in the next few years after reclamation of more land from the sea (which is a constant activity on this island), the street will be extended and assume a few more names.

I hear you ask, so how do people get their mail here? The answer is by post office box. Your mail comes to your employer, who has a P. O. Box number. Now this poses another problem altogether when a courier has to deliver a package. You see, they demand a street address prior to accepting a package for delivery. So you explain to them that there are no street addresses here and that what they need to do is, when the package arrives, give the recipient a call and he or she will direct them to the proper destination.

For example, in my case, come three miles south on the road that runs parallel to the row of pylons on the west side of the city, at that point look out for an old desecrated tire painted white lying on the right side of the road, make a left there and go about two miles till you see a dead camel on your right, turn right and go until you see an old wreck of a rusty brown Toyota Truck. Park there and ask a local where the compound is where most blond women live. Walk to the compound and knock on the door that has a painted number five in English, nine in Arabic and a blue municipality tin plate showing a number three (also in Arabic). Knock hard (the doorbell hasn't worked for the past two years) several times and if you get no response, climb over the perimeter wall of the compound (it is only seven feet tall) by first climbing on the roof of a nearby parked car and knock on the large wooden entrance door of the villa marked with number four in English. (Note: Don't expect a tip, it is against local tradition.)

Wait. I hear a knock on the door. I think my courier package of Christmas cake that I ordered around Easter has arrived. See you.

19

SAFESTWAY

Did you know that at Hancock Secondary School in Mississippi there is actually a McDonald's in the high school? Those unmistakable golden arches keep breaking new ground and are now world-renowned. Well, almost everywhere except in Paris and in some parts of the Arabian world. You see, the Parisians consider yellow as rather tacky and painted the arches of big M in white. Those Frenchmen, they are always trying to be different. The Arabs, on the other hand, are a step ahead of them.

Here in Arabia we have a facility that looks every bit like a McDonald's and when once I took my two kids (without the wife, since she refuses to eat any food that looks like someone sat on it) there for an exciting double cheeseburger meal, we discovered that they only sell kebabs and hummus. Tears rolled down my kids' cheeks and a super-sized kebab dish and a fluffy camel toy did nothing to soothe their troubled souls.

We also have places that are replicas of KFC, Popeye's, Pizza Hut and Wendy's but these stores specialize in local cuisine: shawarma (kind of a wrap sandwich), hummus and kebabs. While much advancement has reached the shores of Arabia, the protection of intellectual property through copyright is not included. If you ever were foolish enough to question it, then be ready to be enlightened by a speech that Arabia, being the cradle of almost all ancient civilizations, gave birth to all of today's inventions and ideas, and thus has a claim on all intellectual properties. Go figure.

Now I have to admit that my interest is not as much in those places that are blatantly ignoring international copyright law as it is in those people who show a little ingenuity. Let me explain. Our supermarket in Dubai where we often go to buy all that stuff we would normally buy at a Safeway back in Vancouver is called, as mentioned earlier, Safestway. You see, the nationals here wanted to be a little better than their counterparts in the western world. Obviously, the Safestway at least sounds better or safer than the Safeway, wouldn't you agree? Now it's an entirely different matter that the red 'S' logo of the Safestway looks identical to the one Safeway uses.

Confused? Don't be. Just remember their claim as an ancient civilization.

The other day my wife bought a magazine called *Bon Appetit*. I am sure you have seen such a magazine on your bookstore's bookshelves because it is a world-renowned magazine on food and wine. The one she bought had Arabic food recipes, advertisements offered by local food stores, and nothing to do with international cuisine or alcoholic wines. On closer examination I discovered that the magazine my wife had bought is really a locally produced magazine except its cover and name is every bit like the internationally acclaimed gourmet food magazine called *Bon Appetit*. I am not sure if the French will feel outraged about this blatant misuse of their magazine or flattered that their brand names are as much in demand as those of North America—*the land of brand equity development.*

Talking about food and wine, one of our favorite watering holes in Abu Dhabi is the Hilton Jazz Club. You ask why? The answer is simple. It is the only jazz club in the city. Sitting at the bar with the one who must be spoken to with a bowed head, we ordered Bacardi (rum to those who have not yet been introduced to the finer ways of living) on the rocks with coke. The coke can looked every bit like an all-American Coca Cola can, but the label read Mecca Cola. Not only that, the can had a warning written on it—*Do not mix with alcohol.*

Well, there was no way I could resist showing the warning on the can to the Egyptian bartender and raising my eyebrows in quick succession. He grabbed my can and looked at it as if this was the first time he had seen that brand and asked in a hushed tone, "Are you a Muslim?" "Nah," I answered in a voice that really said, "Do I look like one?" "The warning is for Muslims, you can use it with your rum," he answered matter-of-factly.

Now we all know what a Starbucks coffee shop looks like (You don't? Where have you been? I think you missed the train.), except when you are in Arabia where some of the coffee shops look exactly like a Starbucks but are named Starcup. Why do they do this, you may ask. Trust me when I tell you it is not because of lack of imagination but it rather is because they can do it. Well, yes, the lack of regional regulatory control gives them that extra degree of freedom but it is more than that. To be exact it is…let me see if the following story can illustrate it better.

One afternoon, my better half took my brown leather wallet for a walk through the myriad expensive designer clothing shops in one of our local enormous, glittering malls, as I sat in a large Starbucks (yeah, it was a Starbucks and not a Starcup) coffee house sipping a piping hot cappuccino. An unassuming Arab walked in and the following conversation commenced between the Arab and a broken English-speaking Filipino clerk behind the counter:

Arab: "I would like one."

Clerk: "Yes Sir?"

Arab: "I want one."

Clerk: "Sorry, Sir. Which one?"

Such conversations are an everyday occurrence in the local shops because of the language barrier and the master/slave relationship between the nationals and imported labor, but my interest was piqued because I could smell a story afoot.

Arab: "One." I could now detect irritation in the Arab's voice for not being able to make the clerk understand his demand.

Frustrated but fearful, the clerk stammered, "A cappuccino, Americana, Mocha, Frappe…which one, Sir?"

The mystery was finally revealed when the Arab, with a sweeping gesture of his right hand, explained that he wanted to buy the shop—a Starbucks of his own.

So you see, they can do whatever they want because they have the magic ingredient—money! That comes oozing out of the ground as black gold. If it still hasn't sunk in, just remember that people here understand copyright as their right to copy.

20

DOUBLE TROUBLE

Did you know that the Chinese ideogram for 'trouble' depicts two women living under one roof? Well, in Arabia under the Islamic law a man can have as many as four wives at any one given time. I guess if two wives mean trouble then four wives would be double trouble.

I am sure that most men, at least the brave ones, would agree with me that living with a woman is nothing less than a challenge. So why allow two wives to a man when it is a given, as clearly explained by the Chinese, that it is going to be trouble, and what were the Arab scholars thinking when they approved four wives to a man? It only proves one thing and that is hormones have no boundaries. Don't look for a logical explanation and common sense in situations that are primarily governed by hormones. It seems that men from the beginning of time have been slaves to their lust for women and till this day the suffering continues.

Having four wives gives a new meaning to intimate table for two. Have you ever noticed in a restaurant or a bar a quiet corner table set for five? It is rather awkward to invite them over for dinner and set the table for seven. My wife finds it rather arduous to have a conversation with four women about their common house or common husband. Then when the discussion moves on to children, as it often does with Arabs, it becomes quite mind-boggling. Having explained the accomplishments of my daughter and son, we have to sit there and listen for hours about the wonderful achievements of the twelve to sixteen children of their family. And the problem becomes quite complex when every boy's long name always has either Abdullah or Mohammed in it and every girl seems to carry Fatima as one of her names.

I have been constantly reminded by my wife of my lack of observation powers as I often seem to forget to comment on her new nail polish color, gradation in her hair color, new shoes, new dress, earring design, necklace length, I could go on and on. Can you imagine being constantly badgered by four wives? I admire the tenacity of Arab men.

But this is supposed to be the land of scholars, mathematicians and legendry poets, so how come they made such a blunder allowing men to commit a mistake two times as big as the Chinese and four times as big as anywhere else. Like I said earlier: hormones are the only answer. I would have loved to be a fly on the wall when an Arab tells his wife how much he loves her and is happy with her but he is planning to bring another wife into her home. I wonder how she feels? I bet she feels happy and thanks God that now she can get a few good nights' sleep without hearing him snoring.

It does open up a few new opportunities though, doesn't it? If one knew he was going to have four wives, then one can make a few plans. Let me illustrate. One could make a list of things one desires in a descending order of priority and pick four wives that satisfy the top four priorities. I mean, one decides to have the most beautiful woman regardless of her mental ability. Poof, you get your first wife and you spend your nights with her (and afternoon siestas, of course). Then you desire someone who could be a gourmet cook and splash, you could go out and get yourself a second wife who could cook you the tastiest meals and you could have dinners with her. You yearn for travel with a private guide. No problem, marry a linguist as your third wife and you never have to feel like a stranger in a foreign country. For the fourth wife, you could choose a doctor because you know that while keeping four wives happy you are going to need a lot of medical attention.

I wonder how mixed-gender marriages would work here. I mean, could the day come when they are liberal enough to allow you to have two female and two male spouses, or how about four male spouses, then one could have a personal five-a-side team of his own. I mean the possibilities are endless.

But what I hear from my Arab friends is that this old tradition of multiple wives is dying. Most modern men in Arabia now prefer to have only one wife at a time. Why does one have to marry more than one when the Natasha content here is so high? You haven't heard of the Natasha content? Don't ever admit that, at least not in a bar to other men. Think of pretty Russian women who want to become your best friend provided you have money to spend on them. No, expand your imagination and you'll get it. Okay, so where was I? Oh yeah, four wives. The demise of the multiple wives tradition has nothing to do with the rights of women, it has more to do with simple economics. One wife is considered expensive, two are a financial liability, three a financial disaster, and four certainly bring about the collapse of one's sanity.

It seems that nature always provides self-correcting situations in disastrous scenarios such as multiple wives. Divorces in Arabia are extremely easy and simple and not as expensive and of such disastrous consequences for men as back in the western world. All a man has to do is say three times, 'I divorce you,' and bingo, you are divorced. Really, that is all there is to it. If you are not one with enough courage to face the wife and utter those simple words three times then today modern technology provides an even simpler solution. You can text her on your mobile phone three times, 'I divorce you,' and bingo, it is all very legal. You are divorced.

I was once told that Arab men never sleep with prostitutes. Well, they offer to marry them then make love and in the morning when leaving, say those magic words three times and they are divorced. So you see, they always sleep with their wives.

Is something telling you that the concept of multiple wives and these simple divorce procedure rules were made by a man? Well, thank God that sensible thinking finally prevailed and the men are swiftly moving towards single-wife scenarios. I bet the cost of housing, transportation, and food has reduced considerably. Just think about it. At ten dollars a pop and another ten for popcorn, chocolate and drinks, going to a cinema for a multiple-wives family with children could cost as much as four hundred dollars per movie. Now with a single wife and a couple of kids, one could go to the movies every week for five weeks for the same budget.

China has one of the oldest civilizations on earth and if Arab men had paid a little attention to the Chinese culture, they would have figured out a lot earlier that multiple women under one roof spells nothing but trouble, just like all those Chinese did several centuries ago.

Somewhere there is going to be a sudden, tremendous surplus of women. Would you pass this message on to e-Harmony? Thanks.

21

ECONOMY IS FOR LOSERS

I once read somewhere that donkeys kill more people annually than plane crashes. No, I lie. I actually saw it on the National Geographic channel and they don't lie, do they? It may be so but on certain occasions when flying in Arabia, I would have rather chosen a donkey-ride. Whatever you do, never fly economy class in the Middle East. It is well worth it to pay oodles of extra money to avoid the economy class hardships. I learned this the hard way and you are lucky to get this invaluable information without suffering the inherent pain that comes with economy class.

First of all, there is no concept of queuing at the ticket counter (British readers should take note of this). While all expatriates will remember their colonial teachings and will line up nice and tidy, all the locals will just walk right past you and push themselves into the front. They may even interrupt the person who is being served and demand immediate attention. I know what you are thinking. You are thinking, why don't the expatriates have some backbone and tell those pushy locals to back off. They don't because they don't want to be imprisoned for seven days and receive twenty lashes everyday of their imprisonment by upsetting some stand-up local citizen who is merely exercising his birthright—*he comes first in his country.*

So you wait. It is less painful than prison. You will have to trust me on this. Once I had to fly from Riyadh to Abu Dhabi on a business trip and waited in a queue for a long time and finally when I reached the counter, the clerk refused to accept my ticket. By mistake the agent had put Mrs. instead of Mr. in front of my name. I explained that I didn't steal the ticket from my lady but he wouldn't believe me. Finally he made a call to confirm that it was my ticket. Actually he insisted on making two calls (at my expense): one to the ticket agent who had issued my ticket and another to my wife.

Once the matter was clear that I was the owner of the ticket, he informed me that the flight was cancelled and a replacement flight was not due for another eight hours. I asked him to endorse my ticket so I could fly on another airline that had a plane leaving in four hours. He smiled and said, "Gladly, sir. I will cancel it but you have to take it to the main office to get it transferred over to the other airline."

He cancelled my ticket and then told me that the office he spoke of was more than fifty kilometers away in town. The taxi ride there and back would have meant two hours' time and $65 in fares. I requested he leave me on their replacement flight, to which he answered, "Too late for that. Your ticket is cancelled."

He didn't have to ask me to move over as two locals arrived and they pushed me away to thrust their tickets on the counter. Ouch, boy, do they have pointy elbows. I took a taxi and went to a downtown office only to discover that it was a prayer break and I must wait for thirty minutes. That I did. The office reopened but the manager was taking a nap at home after the prayers and I was told to wait some more. After another hour wait the manager arrived and grudgingly agreed to change my ticket. All the time he worked on my ticket, a total of twenty minutes, he made me feel as if I was the worst troublemaker he ever had to deal with. I grabbed my new ticket and bolted out of his office to my taxi, the driver of which was quite happy to wait as his meter was still running.

I promised him a big tip if he could get me to the airport in time to catch my flight. That he did. Now $85 lighter with only thirty minutes to spare, I charged towards the ticket counter and jumped the queue to get to the front. You should have seen those stern looks on the faces of the expatriates. They were ready to kill me and I kept apologizing. The agent looked at my ticket and shook his head from side-to-side, saying, "I'm sorry, sir, but this flight has already left."

"But there is still thirty minutes to go," I protested as my hands balled up in tight fists.

"All the passengers were here so we let the flight go. We didn't know about you. No more flights, you take taxi. Go to Dhahran. There is a flight there to Abu Dhabi. But hurry, you don't have much time."

With that explanation he proceeded to order a cup of tea for himself and rubbed his temples. That was too much hard work, looking after customers like me who keep changing their flights. So my alternative turned out to be a several hundred-dollar and over 500-kilometer taxi ride. The taxi driver, convinced that his God was helping him by taking oodles of easy money from me, floored the accelerator. I guess he wanted to see what else his God (or the local airlines) had in store for him.

Clocking at 200 kilometers an hour he started to tell me his life story. Every time he took his hands off the wheel to make a gesture, my life flashed in front of my eyes. I didn't want to insult his driving skills by asking him to slow down so I watched the road for him. Luckily, I managed to warn him of a bunch of camels I could see in the distance and we did slow down just before we had a flat. I shudder to think what would have happened if we had hit one of those one-ton beasts at 200 kilometers an hour. The taxi driver kept thanking his God for putting camels in his way, making him slow down, and I kept complaining to my God for putting me in his taxi

Finally we reached Dhahran Airport, allowing me to catch a flight to Abu Dhabi. On our flight was an old local man who had never seen a plane before but had heard of buses. He thought he was on a fast bus as we started to taxi down the runway but all hell broke loose as soon as we were airborne. He thought he was on his journey to meet his maker. He started to shout and cry in disbelief that infidels like me were accompanying him to his heavenly abode.

You see, he was not afraid of dying, he was afraid of dying with me being close to him. Some people are so picky. His family finally managed to calm him down by promising him that I was going only as far as Abu Dhabi and would not accompany him to his final destination.

And finally when I did reach Abu Dhabi and called up my supervisor, he sympathized with me and told me I didn't have to hurry as the meeting was cancelled due to an unscheduled holiday announced by the government that day.

Economy is for losers.

22

IN SEARCH OF AN ADVENTURE

I had hardly taken a sip of my first cup of coffee when the one who wants me to be fit enough to compete in the Olympics walks in and sits in front of me and announces, "Guess what? I just had a great idea."

Now you will appreciate that at seven in the morning, the brain of any reasonable person is just beginning to limber up and one is gently whispering to the clouds in one's coffee, 'Good Morning.' To jump out of one's chair, shouting, 'I just had a great idea,' is not only hard for one to believe, but is rather uncivilized, don't you agree? I see, you can't answer because someone is around. That's okay.

"Two other ladies and I are planning to drive through the middle of the world's harshest and most treacherous desert and we need you in case the truck gets stuck in sand.

What do you say? It would be so much fun, what an adventure."

Right. You know what I was thinking at this moment so I won't mention it here. However, with the grace of God I had an excuse, a damn good one to boot, as I answered with sorrowful eyes (I was pretending, okay?), "Honey, I have to go on a business trip to Sana'a in Yemen this week. I am so sorry. But you girls should go. And don't worry about the truck for it won't get stuck. They are built for that sort of thing. Just stay on compact sand trails and don't climb too many steep dunes."

Without probing further (or wasting time, as she would put it), she reluctantly agreed to go on without me. Although I was half-hearted before about going on a business trip to Yemen (because of the constant danger of people being kidnapped or shot at), now I was determined to go. I'd rather face bullets than...never mind. Digging a truck out of sand under the hot Arabian sun just didn't appeal to my sensibilities. You know what I mean.

So, the following Saturday (the first day of an Arabian week), as my lady and her friends in their khakis set off to answer the call of the desolate desert, I took a flight out to Sana'a. Upon arrival in Sana'a I discovered that my Vice President from

Canada had cancelled the meeting due to some sudden and mysterious illness. *Chickening out, more like it*, I thought. Smart man. But now the dilemma I faced was where to go for the next three to four days. It was simply too dangerous to venture outside the hotel and staying there for four days was, well, rather dull. I daren't return back home too quickly in case my lady had postponed her visit by a day or so, besides, I would feel guilty sitting at home gulping down chilled beer while I had told her I wouldn't be there.

An amazing thought occurred to me (it is known to happen now and then). I wondered if I should try on my own to go on an adventure trip. Because if I liked it then I could, you know, be more of a partner to my lady…at least it sure would impress her. So, charged with this unfamiliar but exhilarating feeling, I contacted the tour operator in the hotel and asked him what adventure he could send me on (as long as it was out of Yemen). I still didn't fancy being kidnapped or shot at.

The next morning I was on a flight to Egypt on a three-day tour of Cairo and Luxor. Wow, the land of the Pharaohs and there I was on my own, venturing out on an exciting trip. I landed at the Cairo airport and as my taxi hurtled towards my three-star hotel, my heart sank. The city was dirty and the people looked angry and inhospitable. I took a deep breath and told myself to open my mind's eye to see adventure in the poverty and misery.

I waited in the lobby for a good twenty minutes but could not make myself noticed by the reception clerk. He was busy sorting out a dozen or so Japanese tourists who seemed to be complaining about overcharges. There was a feeling of dismay in my head but expectation of adventure was smoldering in my heart. As luck would have it the concierge came over to me and asked me if I was at the right hotel or needed help, or something to that effect, since my Arabic is bad and his English was non-existent.

He reached for my small suitcase and gestured for me to follow him. He opened a room on the second floor and placed my suitcase on the bed. I was impressed with such treatment, to forego the formality of checking in and moving into a room straightaway. I offered him a generous tip and he gave me a big smile in return, things were beginning to look up. I opened my suitcase and decided to take a shower. The room was clean and so was the shower room. I had a long shower and then wrapped a hotel towel around my waist. I was impressed to see that a three-star hotel also provided small packages of shampoo, conditioner and a bottle of very expensive aftershave, *KOUROS* from Yves Saint Laurent. I applied a generous helping of the *KOUROS* and sat out on the balcony with nothing but my towel wrapped around me.

Now, I should've noticed that something was not quite kosher about all this. Because just as I relaxed in my chair on the balcony I heard someone come through the door. I turned around and ran into the room to find two burly men staring at me: an Egyptian and a Syrian, as I later found out. They started to scream at me in Arabic and one of them called hotel security. Two large security men with a guard dog appeared. The concierge had misunderstood me and put me in an already occupied room…I guess that must be evident to you by now. The Syrian accused me of being a burglar and no matter how much I explained that burglars aren't in the habit of stripping and wandering around on balconies in a towel, none of it mattered. Actually it became worse when security checked at the front desk and found I was not a guest of the hotel—*I had never checked in*. Of course, the concierge's shift had finished and he was nowhere to be seen.

Suddenly, the guard dog jumped toward me and instinctively I jumped away and onto the bed thinking the dog was going to pull off my towel and make me show all my jewels. But instead the dog tried to get under the bed where, when the guards searched, they found the Syrian's small briefcase with some illegal drugs in it. Needless to say, at that very instant I turned into a hero in the eyes of the hotel management and they offered me a free stay and free use of a chauffeur-driven hotel car. I was delighted and immediately changed into my clothes and took advantage of the hotel's free transportation, went straight to the airport and found a flight back home.

I decided that digging a stuck truck out of sand under the hot Arabian sun was a safer adventure than spending the night wrapped in a towel with two Arab strangers in their hotel room. Actually, when you come to think of it, I did have a rather exciting experience, otherwise I wouldn't be writing about it. Oh, here comes my wife, "Hey honey, want to go dune-bashing?"

23

NO BARKING

If you are like me in reading every scrap of news in the local newspapers, you will find that life around you is full of odd but humorous happenings. Here is one I read about the other day. A large, local corporation has embarked on a multi-million dollar, marketing campaign for their products and to support this they offered a lot of promotional gifts in their 'Scratch & Win' contest. So what was odd about it? Well, the contest was publicized as 'Scratch & Lose.'

I just couldn't resist and so called up their marketing department to ask about their innovative program. A serious voice on the other end of the phone explained to me that most if not all such marketing gimmicks, as he put it, of 'Scratch & Win' in the west don't really offer much of a gift. He further explained that most people who fall for it lose money. Because the owner of the company in question was not allowed, in accordance with his religious beliefs, to lie to anyone, including his customers, he decided to go the truthful way: 'Scratch & Lose.' I decided not to ask him any embarrassing questions like if the marketing campaign had shown an improvement in sales.

Here is another one. A news item read that the numbers at the suicide attack training camps in Iraq are rapidly dwindling. See what I mean? How could anyone survive and live to apply his training skills if one is training to be a suicide attacker? I mean aren't you dead if you are well trained? Well, I guess one isn't expected to be too smart if one has chosen suicide attacker as his/her career. In the west I can't imagine this to be a flourishing career since no firm in their right mind is going to admit you into the training camp without indemnity insurance, life insurance, worker's compensation insurance and at least two references from your previous employers…I mean, the old work practices die hard, don't they?

Only recently I came upon a news item that was intriguing. It had a picture that showed a man pulling a van tied to his moustache. The news item explained that he could also lift 17 bricks with his moustache and was hoping to pull an aircraft soon. Let me take a pause to breathe. Why? Why on earth one would want to pull an aircraft with his moustache. When I posed this question at a dinner party to my daughter's Physical Education teacher, she said that women would never do something like this. Do you think she missed something here or maybe she knows a few women with moustaches that I have missed?

Talk about bad luck. One of the newspapers reported a man had been robbed of his mobile phone. The man gave robbers a chase and was stopped by three plain-clothes policemen traveling in an unmarked car. Police demanded his identity papers and as he took out his wallet the three men grabbed his wallet and fled, they were robbers too. I bet that poor man wished he never got out of bed that morning.

My favorite stories involve novel flying experiences. A 32-year-old housewife, whose husband was working in Qatar as an engineer, flew out from the southern Indian city of Kochi to Doha to join her husband. Now what you need to know here is that according to newspapers this was her maiden flight and she was terrified of flying. When she boarded the plane she tried to find ways to alleviate her fear of flying and finally managed to put herself to sleep. She was in such a deep sleep that she had no idea that her plane had landed, disembarked all passengers, took on new crew and new passengers, and flew back to Kochi. Air India, obviously embarrassed by their mistake, gave her a free ticket to fly again to Doha. Mind you, this time she actually enjoyed her flight because she claimed she had done this kind of thing once before. Good for her.

In another newspaper report I read a story that was simply amazing. In an economy class of Air India a woman passenger asked the airhostess if she could bring her a glass of milk. Once the milk arrived, the passenger in question opened her handbag, took out a long snake and proceeded to feed milk to the snake. Can you imagine the horror on the faces of passengers sitting close to her? They called the airhostess back and complained. The snake-passenger assured the airhostess and other passengers that the snake was her pet and quite harmless, provided that people didn't panic and upset him. Well, as I don't have to tell you, people panicked. In the ensuing shouting and confusion, the snake escaped, slithered down to the floor and disappeared.

People undid their seatbelts and stood on their seats. Would you believe it, at exactly that time the plane hit turbulence and the airhostess started shouting, asking the passengers to sit back down and fasten their seatbelts. Do you think passengers sat back and strapped themselves to their seats? Like hell they did. I guess people would rather have a few bumps on their heads than die of snakebite. Well, finally the owner found the pet snake and had to travel with it for the remainder of the flight in a washroom. That caused an emergency of another nature. A lot of passengers finished their journey sitting cross-legged. When the plane finally landed there was a mad dash for the airport washrooms.

And the last story is actually what once happened to me. I drove to a parking lot in Saudi Arabia and found only one empty space. I parked my car there and went about my business. About an hour later when I came back I found a very agitated Arab who bitterly complained about me parking my car in his designated parking space. I shrugged my shoulders and said, "I didn't know. There aren't any signs saying that it is a reserved space. I'm so sorry."

To which he pointed his finger to the wall facing my car and said, "Can't you read what it says there on the wall?" I looked and saw the sign that I had noticed before but couldn't understand. It read: 'No Barking.'

Later I discovered that there is no 'P' sound in the Arabic language and they pronounce the 'P' sound as 'B' and I guess they follow the same practice when they write.

I remember once visiting my newly made Arab friend who, when I introduced him to my wife, asked me, "You beat her?" Shocked and perplexed, I stared at my wife and then at him and said, "No. What made you ask that?"

"I'm Abdullah and you beat her?" he asked politely. Just then the light dawned on me. Somehow he thought my name was Peter and he was trying to confirm it. From that point on I thanked God for my parents not naming me Peter.

Oops! I told you one more story than I intended to. I think I hear my wife's car outside. Now, if you will excuse me, I have to go and help my lady with the barking.

24

THE WILD WEST

Making a business call in the rural part of Saudi Arabia gives new meaning to adventure. Or maybe a more fitting word would be frustration or annoyance, but for now let us call it adventure and I'd let you decide what it ought to be called.

While I was working as a consultant for a large corporation in Saudi Arabia, its technical services department asked me to visit one of their clients, called Mohammed, who was having low production and poor work efficiency problems. The client was located in a small town in a place called Bul Jouroshi up in the Sarawat Mountains in the southwest of Saudi Arabia. The company provided me with the client's contact numbers and asked me to make my own travel arrangements.

I called the owner and arranged a date and later on confirmed it by a fax message. I asked him if there were any five-star hotels and to my surprise he said yes. I asked him to book me a room and he told me not to worry and said he himself would come to the airport to pick me up.

One Tuesday evening I arrived from Riyadh by the Saudi Airlines to the airport that was thirty miles from the town of Bul Jouroshi. It was a small airport and soon after our arrival, about twenty of us, all locals (apart from me, of course), quickly disappeared. And there I stood alone in a small eerie airport. My host never turned up. I saw a policeman closing the airport and asked him how I could get to town. With a straight face he told me that it was too late to find any transportation and I would have to walk. I politely asked him if he could give me a ride and he said he lived in a small house right next to the airport. I pleaded with him to let me use his telephone, to that he agreed. I called Mohammed.

He sounded surprised that I was at the airport and he complained, asking why I didn't call him before I left Riyadh. I reminded him of my fax and confirmed date, to which he paid no attention and said he had visitors and no way could he come to pick me up. He told me to wait by the curb outside the airport and assured me that I would find a ride and then he put the phone down.

Shucks!

I sat by the curb and watched the sun going down. Suddenly, and out of nowhere, a small Toyota pickup truck loaded with sheep in the back pulled over and asked me if I wanted a ride. I loosened my necktie knot and nodded yes. He said $200 and I nodded yes again. I slipped in next to him and he took off toward the mountains. We had gone only about ten miles when he stopped, got out of his truck, walked down a gravel path and disappeared. I waited for about twenty minutes wondering what was going on. I looked at the goats to see if they felt panic. No they were just fine, it was only I. I got out of the truck and decided to go down the same path that the driver took to see if I could find him. I didn't have to go far when I spotted him with a few people. A feeling of terror passed through my body and I wondered if they were contemplating murdering me. Not paranoid, just cautious. And then I noticed that they were actually praying. That was a good thing. I rushed back to the truck and sat there quietly awaiting his return.

Ten minutes later the man came back and off we went towards town. Once we arrived, I requested the truck owner to take me to any of the five-star hotels. He explained in his broken English that there was only one and then he drove me there. I looked at what some would call a hole-in-the-wall hotel with a huge signboard that read: 'Five Star Hotel.' On inspection I found a small room with broken, stone flooring, a small, dirty sink and a cot and that was the deluxe room.

I asked the hotel owner if there were any true five-star hotels in town, to which he inquired, "You mean like…Ramada Inn?"

You can imagine my surprise and with slackened jaw I muttered, "You've a Ramada Inn in this town? Like in Ramada Inn from the USA?"

"Sure we do." He instructed my Toyota pick-up buddy how to get to Ramada Inn. My buddy looked at me and said, "That is ten miles out of town. It'll cost you another $200, okay?"

As if I had a choice. Okay it was. I was tired and besides I was on company expense. I jumped back in the truck and away we went to find Ramada Inn. Perched on top of a mountain was a large resort hotel with a familiar logo and sign announcing the *Ramada Inn*. I couldn't believe my luck.

It was dark but there was a clerk behind the reception desk who looked more like security staff. I asked, "This is Ramada Inn, like Ramada Inn in the USA?"

"Yes sir," came back the short reply with a big smile.

"And you have lots of five-star quality rooms?"

"You're right. We do have hundreds of rooms, sir."

"May I have a room, please?"

"No sir." His smile was still firmly planted as he explained, "We are not open for business yet, sir."

After a lot of pleading and begging ($100 helped too), he let me sleep on a kitchen counter (the hotel was not yet furnished). Another twenty dollars got me a sandwich and a non-alcoholic beer.

The next morning I called Mohammed, who came in his shiny Mercedes to pick me up and took me straight to his factory. He ranted on about how my company, owned by the Saudi government, was not providing him financial help, especially when his manufacturing plant was unable to operate at high utilization rates. You see the plant was designed based on technical advice from us, so he felt he had a legitimate claim.

At his facility I spent some time talking with operators and learned that every year the owner took four months' summer vacation, fired all the staff and shut down the facility. Then he took another two months to hire new staff and went back into production. When I confronted Mohammed with these facts he simply shook his head and said, "You should have taken my vacation into account when you designed my facility."

Upon my return I made my report recommending Mohammed be dropped from our customer list. To this Mohammed complained and made a call to one of his cousins at the ministry of industry. The Company quickly fired me and promised to compensate Mohammed annually.

I have every intention of returning to Bul Jouroshi, not to confront Mohammed again but to enjoy a weekend at the new Ramada Inn…when or maybe if it opens.

25

ONCE IN A LIFETIME

Constant change is what the wanderer spirit yearns for. Or is it some quirk in our brains that eggs us on to seek change, even when we might be living in a perfect environment? I'm sorry, I didn't mean to open this story with dull philosophy, but there comes a moment in everyone's life when change is the only answer. How do we know when that moment arrives? I don't know about you but in my case it's easy— the one who possesses the wisdom of living and dying (and not necessarily in that order) tells me when.

And it was when! So it was no surprise to me that my lady on the 'when day' announced that she missed spring flowers and had purchased a holiday package for us to go for a week to the lush, green rolling hills of Paphos in the southwest of Cyprus. Now I have nothing against Cyprus but it is one of those places that can be better described as a 'once-in-a-lifetime' holiday destination, i.e.

once there, no need to ever go back. Maybe the following explanation would help.

We arrived at the Larnaca International Airport and went to pick up our economy-sized cheap car rental. The salesman gave us the look that says, 'Ah ha, another sucker,' and said, "Would you like the free upgrade to a 4X4 SUV with soft top?"

"Wow," is the only thing my wife uttered before signing the papers and a few minutes later we sat in a dirty, old, soft-top SUV. No matter what we did, we could not make the soft top retract. When we complained, the salesman grunted, "It's a free upgrade, what do you expect, miracles?" As we gunned our mighty SUV down the highway to Paphos, it refused to engage in high gear. Grinding ahead in third gear, revving the engine at 4000 rpm, we had no idea if we had enough gas to make it since the gauge was stuck on full.

Thank God, we made it to Paphos at dusk and started to look around for a hotel to check in. We had decided not to pre-book any hotel in order to experience the true spirit of adventure. Now here is a dilemma I don't know how to resolve. My theory that holidays are meant for rest and relaxation is directly opposite to my wife's view that holidays are meant for pain and suffering.

Sorry, she calls it fun and adventure. After checking out several hotels that were either closed or full (mostly closed), we went to an information office and picked up a hotel guide. We browsed the brochure and liked the looks of a three-star, sea-facing hotel advertised for sixty-five dollars a night. It took us only forty-five minutes to find the three-blocks-away hotel (thankfully we had the help of an information office and a map) and asked the reception clerk how much. One hundred and sixty-five American dollars a night, was her answer in a tone that firmly implied 'take it or leave it.'

We showed her our pamphlet and sixty-five dollar deal and she called her manager. He explained that the sixty-five dollar offer was a special that could not be offered over the counter, it must be booked by phone. I looked at him as one would look at a man holding out two open palms with a coin in one, asking which one. I pulled out my cell phone and dialed the hotel number. The desk phone on the counter rang and the manager picked it up. Now we were having a chat face-to-face, but on our phones. I asked for the rate, the manager said sixty-five dollars, and we made the booking. I know it sounds ridiculous but then remember you are dealing with people who are taught to blindly follow the rules and not necessarily to apply logic.

Once we put our melting cheeses and butter in the mini fridge and settled into our room, the cleaning lady arrived. We told her to come back later, to which she responded by turning on a large, industrial-sized vacuum cleaner and turning on the TV for her viewing pleasure as she vacuumed our room with no regard to our presence. She replenished our mini fridge with two water bottles and slammed the door behind her. A few minutes later the manager called and informed us that the rate was now changed to seventy dollars and when we asked why, he responded that we were using their mini fridge by putting our cheeses in it and that would cost extra. Once we informed him that we were sorry and had removed our food from their fridge, he came upstairs to inspect the fridge and once satisfied that we indeed had removed our cheeses he went back to reception and removed the five-dollar extra charge. As soon as he left our room we put all the stuff back in the fridge. See, logic has nothing to do with it, just rules that could be bend.

Now, here is something else that defies logic. Later that evening when we sat in the hotel restaurant and asked for their best bottle of wine, they told us it was very expensive. While we waited for more information and nothing more came, we asked politely, "Could we have it now, *please*?" Several minutes went by and then the manager came to inform us in a hushed voice that there was only one bottle of expensive wine left and stared us with a blank expression on his face. This was getting not only ridiculous but infuriating so my wife repeated, "Could we have it *now*, please?" It seemed that this threw the manager into a real quandary. Finally he responded, "Okay, it is on the house." As he walked away my wife looked at me as if to ask—*do they do drugs here?*

So we finally had the last bottle of their best wine at no charge and remember these were the same people who wanted an extra five dollars for the use of their mini fridge. Now, I could go on but the whole experience turned out to be full of similar stories that seemed as if someone had designed this place both to confuse you and to test your wits.

Okay, one last story. Upon the return of the rental car, the agent asked us if we had filled up the gas tank. We said yes, but reminded him that the gauge didn't work, to which he responded, "Nor does the mileage-meter." Right. Okay, just one more. On our flight back on Cyprus Airways, we were on a non-stop, direct flight from Larnaca to Dubai that first landed in Bahrain. Worried that something was wrong with the plane or one of the passengers might be ill, we asked an air hostess why a non-stop, direct flight was making a stop in Bahrain? She coolly answered that they were not asking us to change aircraft. While we waited for further enlightenment, she walked away to welcome the newly arriving passengers on our non-stop, direct flight.

See? I did tell you it was a once-in-a-lifetime holiday, didn't I? My advice: Go to Hawaii.

26

CALL OF THE MOUNTAINS

My son, when he was little, believed that his dad was a fearless warrior. He was convinced that when it came to going to McDonald's for a burger, his dad boldly went where no dad had gone before. I always managed to get an extra portion of fries and extra packs of ketchup for my son and that made me a hero in his eyes. But none of that mattered when we were at home because as soon as the one who must not be argued with would walk into my study, my son would instantly know that even heroes must obey their generals and he would quietly leave my study.

The other day while I was enjoying a cold non-alcoholic beer by the pool, my lady wife asked, "Did you know there are mountains in Saudi Arabia?"

"Ah, well, yes dear," I stuttered, trying to figure out where this was leading.

"Why didn't you tell me that? We don't communicate very well, do we?"

I simply looked at her blankly, wondering if a discussion on regional geography was critical to a good marriage.

"Never mind," she continued, "my friends from Yellow Knife, Graham and Judy, are arriving next week and we are taking them to the Saudi mountains. Please arrange it."

Right. Well, I was in luck. I immediately called a friend of mine who works for Saudi Telecom and happened to come from those mountains and he agreed to accompany us and take us around in his Land Cruiser. When her friends arrived we flew to a small town in the foothills of the western mountains and were greeted by my friend Abdullah. He came prepared with Arabic food for several days, camping gear and other necessities and we all climbed aboard for a blissful adventure in the mountains. He was quite taken by a plump, blond Judy in a red polka dot dress.

Our first stop was a beautiful waterfall surrounded by high cliffs, and against the advice of Abdullah, the ladies decided to slip into their bikinis to go for a swim. We men sat on a huge boulder where I shared with them my theory of men as genetically never adventurous enough. There always was a nagging woman behind an adventurous man driving him away from his home.

Suddenly two shots rang out and the sound of bullets ricocheting off the cliff walls echoed through the hills. Abdullah hastily explained that some religious people up in the hills may have spotted our half naked ladies and they were taking pot shots at them. Well, we grabbed the ladies and scooted out of there so fast that we left behind a perfectly laid out and untouched Arabic feast of kebabs, hummus and pita bread.

Now this I don't get. While I was petrified by this experience and suggested, for the safety of us all, that we abandon this trip, my lady laughed and said to Judy, "See what I mean, no sense of adventure. It was fun, wasn't it?" And then they giggled.

Abdullah looked at me and nodded his head as if saying—*I now understand your theory of men*. Needless to say, we moved on and drove along winding mountain roads. Later that evening, Abdullah found us a quiet spot away from any nearby villages and we camped. I must say it was quite magical to sit by a campfire and watch millions of stars hanging above in an unpolluted sky. The sound of silence was magnificent…no gun shots.

The next day we arrived in a small village on their market day. A few Bedouins sitting around in a small village square were selling local, hand-woven carpets. These carpets were, how could I put it politely, crap, utterly useless. My lady decided to buy one to give as a gift to Judy, dressed this time in bright orange polka dots, to take home as a souvenir. Judy was delighted with this gesture and shared that they could not find such art in Yellow Knife. I felt a strong urge to say something about the incredulity of her statement but bit my lip and stayed quiet for the sake of preserving a future with my lady wife.

Within a few minutes there was a crowd of about fifty villagers gathered to watch the game of bartering, a ritual one must follow to demonstrate to his friends that one understands local traditions. My lady wife led the way. The Bedouin asked for 350 Saudi riyals (about $100) for one carpet. This was preposterous, but prices here are fixed according to the way you look and dress. Neatly dressed blond ladies attract the highest prices, closely followed by large, white Americans wearing loud-colored T-shirts and trousers and speaking with a Texan accent. The whole crowd nodded in favor of the Bedouin. My lady countered with a price of 50 riyals (about

$15) and the crowd looked at her with admiration, this time all heads nodded in her favor. The nodding of heads went on for about forty minutes and finally the purchase was made for 125 riyals (about $35) and there was resounding applause from the crowd. While this 'adventure' was going on, we men stood in the intense heat of a blazing Arabian sun, keeping an eye out for Bedouin snipers.

The crunch came the following day when we arrived in a Bedouin village on their weekly goat market day. The chief of this Bedouin village, an old man who looked to be in his late seventies, took a liking to Judy—dressed in a striking yellow polka dot dress—and asked Graham if he could have her for his wife…wife number four. Graham, not knowing any Arabic, simply smiled and nodded. At this point the old man with his steel grip grabbed Judy's arm and started to drag her towards his hut. Abdullah hastily explained to us what had happened and said that was all the old man needed, the approval of Graham, to marry Judy.

At this point I saw both horror and joy in Graham's face. Horror because he didn't know how to go back to Judy's parents and explain to them what happened to their darling daughter, and joy…well, if you don't know why the joy, then obviously you haven't been married for too long. There is no way I can explain this and hope to live happily for the rest of my life so you'll just have to figure it out for yourself.

To our great relief a large Bedouin woman, supposedly the chief's first wife came out with a large piece of wood in her hand and started to beat the old man. His grip loosened and we took Judy then ran from the village as fast as we could.

There is a lesson here: blond ladies in loud polka dot dresses don't mix well with Bedouin chiefs, the Bedouin carpet trade, and Bedouin snipers.

Remember this when you visit the mountains of Saudi Arabia.

27

HEART ATTACK, SERIOUSLY?

Riyadh, the capital of Saudi Arabia, is one of the world's fastest growing cities. Its population has swelled from less than a million in the late 1980s to over four million now. I believe my numbers are correct but if they are a little sketchy then you will have to forgive me. You see I am recovering from a heart attack, I think.

I was working in Riyadh on an assignment and one morning I woke up with pain in my left arm. I dressed and went to the office but the pain persisted and it started to creep towards my left shoulder. One of my colleagues asked me if I was feeling okay. I told him about my pain and he asked if I had any chest pain. I took a deep breath and felt a little discomfort. When I shared that information with my friend, he said it could be a heart attack and I should go to a hospital straightaway.

With beads of perspiration on my forehead, I drove to a hospital (name withheld in an attempt to save future lives), walked up to the emergency reception desk and said, "I need urgent medical attention because I think I'm having a heart attack."

"Who told you that?" asked a burly Jordanian male nurse, chewing on his big moustache.

I looked around to make sure he was talking to me and responded, "No one. I figured it out all by myself. Actually, a friend helped. You see, I have this pain in my arm that seems to be traveling up to my shoulder and I am having a little chest pain. Can I see a specialist?"

"You need to see a specialist," he echoed with authority and then added, "but first I need some information and then you will see an emergency doctor who will give you a referral to see a cardiologist."

It took over thirty minutes (due mainly to a prayer break) to fill out my and my employer's names, those of my father's and his father's, home and work addresses and various contact numbers. The receptionist was not pleased to learn that I was not a Saudi resident. He asked for a promise that I would pay cash and I nodded my approval. In this part of the world the word of honor still has more value than credit cards.

The receptionist escorted me to a cubicle and asked me to wait there. When another twenty minutes lapsed and my chest pain intensified, I went back to the reception desk to make sure they hadn't forgotten about me. The receptionist gave me a stern look and told me to go back to my cubicle. The emergency physician would be there as soon as he came back from his tea break.

Finally an Egyptian doctor strolled into the cubicle, smacking his lips as if savoring the last bit of sweet tea. He had just started asking me questions when a woman rushed into my cubicle and pushed a small baby into the doctor's arms. I thought the doctor would go ballistic with this intrusion but to my dismay he completely ignored me, sitting and clutching my chest, and asked the woman what the problem was. She showed him a plastic container of wet wipes (used to wipe the baby) and hurriedly explained that the baby had somehow managed to open up the top and drank some of the fluid that had gathered at the bottom of the container.

The doctor sniffed and then dipped his finger in and tasted the fluid. He thought for a moment and then put the container to his lips and drank the entire liquid content of the wet-wipes container. Watching that doctor drink it and nothing bad happening to him, the mother took the baby back and calmly left the cubicle.

I looked at the doctor in amazement and he laughed and explained that the fluid contained a lot of alcohol mixed with some detergents. Alcohol is illegal in Saudi Arabia so any amount in any form is welcome. I shuddered at the thought that I had trusted this man with my life.

Listening to my symptoms he agreed that I should see a specialist, but only after some rest. He went back with me to the reception desk and asked the receptionist to check me in for a couple of days and told me not to worry about the $200-a-night room charge as they would collect that from my company. The receptionist explained to the doctor that I was not a Saudi resident and hearing this, the doctor without hesitation told me there was no need for me to stay at the hospital and I could see a specialist straightaway. He asked me if I would pay cash and I made another promise that I would.

The doctor wrote a pink slip and gave it to the receptionist. I waited again and then once again asked the receptionist if I could see the specialist before the heart attack killed me. He rolled his eyes and shouted for a nurse. The receptionist reached for a file folder, wrote a note and gave it to the nurse, asking him to take me to the specialist.

The nurse brought me to a very small office. A man dressed in a white coat with a stethoscope around his neck was sleeping with his head resting on a desk. The nurse coughed and the doctor woke up and rubbed his eyes. He took the file, pointed to a chair across from his desk, and with a casual wave of his hand dismissed the nurse. He looked deep in thought as he read that eight-line message on the note written by the receptionist and read the pink slip at least three times. He kept on shaking his head from side to side.

Finally he walked around the desk and stood by my side. So far no words had been spoken. I thought the tension in the room was enough to give me another heart attack. From his coat pocket he took out a small flashlight and checked my ears. Then he checked inside my nose and proceeded to check my throat. That was too much for me and I asked impatiently, "Why are you checking my ears, nose and throat? I have a pain in my arm and chest. I think I'm having a heart attack, no?"

"It is because I am an ENT specialist. The heart specialist is busy with some VIPs today. Reception has asked me to give you a thorough ENT check-up. Today is the first day of the week so the ENT check-up is only half its normal price. It's a bargain, besides, one of these days you will need a full ENT check-up anyway. How old are you?"

After over two hours in that hospital I was convinced I would have a nervous breakdown before I would die from a heart attack so left and went back to work. I never saw a heart specialist and am happy to report my pain was due to a touch of indigestion.

The hospital name is still withheld in order to save lives.

28

ALADDIN'S GHOST

The other day I visited my wife at her emergency clinic to see her in action. She had often told me that emergency work in the Arabian Gulf countries was far more enjoyable than it was back in Canada and I ought to drop by sometime. You see, in the Gulf countries there are hardly any drug junkies or alcohol-related problems, most emergency cases here are related to auto accidents. From one hundred miles an hour to a dead stop in zero seconds and presto, you are in an emergency room. Severely mangled bodies with limbs severed or mutilations from a crash impact are often challenging for the world of surgical medicine.

But more on this later, for I am sure that we will be touching on the subject of automobiles a few more times before we end our discussion of the Arabian Gulf. Anyway, since I had already seen just about every run and rerun of ER on TV, I decided to come down to my wife's emergency room and witness the real thing.

While I sat at her computer desk surfing for bargain holidays on the net, the front desk nurse escorted a patient into a cubicle directly opposite to where I was sitting. I had a direct view because nobody bothered to completely close the curtains. The man slowly stripped to bare his lower part of the body to the emergency physician in charge, my wife, and pointed at his testicles that, with muscles around it contracting and expanding, were gradually shifting position in the scrotum sack. There was terror in the Arab's eyes and his face showed both panic and mystification. His index finger, moving in small circular motions and retracing the path of the gradually moving testicles, continued to point at his groin as the gaze of his widened eyes followed his fingers. I thought he was going to end up hypnotizing himself.

"Zinh," he whispered in a slow and nervous tone.

My wife gave an inquisitive look to the interpreter who explained to her that the patient believed a Zinh or ghost had entered into his body and was moving around in his testicles. He wanted the doctor to perform an exorcism to drive the

Zinh out of his testicles. I moved a little closer to the cubicle and was certain it was some kind of a joke, but obviously not to the old man who continued to point out Zinh in his testicles. My wife was trying so hard to suppress her laughter that tiny tears escaped from the corners of her eyes. She took a small hammer-like instrument and lifted it above her head, threatening to bring it down with force.

This horrified the patient even more. It looked as if he was expecting sympathy, a gentle massage of his testicles, perhaps, rather than a beating. My wife looked at the interpreter and asked him to tell the patient that he should go home and have a long, hot bath. And if that didn't work then for him to come back and she would beat the Zinh out of his testicles with her hammer.

Now, don't shake your head, the story is true. Let me share a little more on this subject. There are two types of Zinh: good ones and bad ones. Remember the Zinh (or genie, as we remember it in the west) in the magic lamp of Aladdin, son of Mustapha the tailor? *Aladdin*…what do you mean, you haven't heard of him. He came from the *Tales from the Arabian Nights*. Remember now? *Aladdin*, you know, from Persia? No, no, not from Baghdad. Saddam Hussein was from Baghdad. Aladdin came from Persia. Oh, never mind, you'll figure it out, just watch CNN.

Anyway, Aladdin's Zinh was a good one because he always obeyed and rescued his master from grave perils. The bad Zinh does things like get into the testicles and frighten little old men.

There is a sporty Zinh, too. Tariq, my business development manager in Saudi Arabia who happens to be a Saudi, once told me that he never liked his soccer team playing in Oman because in Oman, there are two Zinhs who are very good at soccer and they always score goals against the Saudi team. You can only see these rarely and they appear as fleeting flashes of light under the bright Arabian sun. They are always helping the Oman soccer team by curving straight shots into the Saudi soccer team net. I guess Tariq has never seen *Bend it like Beckhem* movie.

At this point you may be wondering if there are any good Zinhs in these modern times. Well, according to Tariq, they certainly exist. I know I was not so sure at first either until he demonstrated to me the powers of the good Zinh. This is what happened. Tariq's uncle knows a good Zinh who always accompanies him on his visits to car rental agencies to help him get a good discount. To experience this firsthand, Tariq, his uncle and I went to a local Hertz dealer and I asked for a rental car for the weekend. The uncle suddenly stood up, placed his walking cane in a corner against a wall, and sat back in his chair. He looked sternly at the dealer and hissed in a low voice, "If you don't give a good discount to my friend, I will ask my Zinh to pick up that stick and beat you to a pulp."

The car dealer nervously looked at the uncle and the stick. And then it happened. The stick moved and gradually slid down to the floor. The uncle picked up the stick, raised it over his head and roared, "Do you really want to get beaten? Give him a discount or I'll ask the Zinh to pummel you!"

That did it. The car dealer quickly nodded and offered me a fifty-percent discount. Did the uncle, being six foot four and 300 pounds, in an angry mood to boot, have anything to do with it? That I don't know. All I know is that thereafter every time I visited him in his house, his cane in a corner kept sliding off the wall as he placed it just at the right inclination where gravity would do its job. Practice makes perfect. And obviously the perfect man deserves good Zinhs.

I wish I knew good Zinhs when I was raising my two kids. It would have been so much easier to control my kids by threatening them with my good buddy Zinh rather than groveling before them at every meal, asking, "Would you eat just one more spoonful? This one is for Daddy, honey."

Wait a minute. What was that? I thought I felt something move in my trousers.

29

LOST IN TRANSLATION

Here is a riddle for you. What do you give the lady who has everything? The answer is Penicillin. I am sorry, that was in poor taste. The one I really wanted to ask you is what does one do when one has accumulated an unimaginable amount of money. The answer is simple: whatever the heck one desires.

There is no better place, in my humble opinion, to illustrate my point than here in the oil-rich Arabian countries. Consider this. During the first Gulf invasion one such Arabian country vowed to fight to the bitter end and till the last drop of blood and to do so they gave the contract to the Pakistani army. See what I mean? And when they do train their army, some peculiar challenges emerge. For instance, most of the locals hired for military service only speak Arabic and, of course, the military advisors are from the crack army units of the US and the UK and they don't speak a word of Arabic.

No problem. The answer is translators. Or is it? Such translators are hired from those Middle Eastern countries where English-speaking tourist guides are frequently employed.

This is how it works. During combat training, an instructor gives an urgent command and the translator then thinks about it for a few minutes, mulls it over (to make sure he has got it right), and then translates it to the best of his ability (limited by his own knowledge of the English language he learned while working as a tourist guide in his country) to the soldiers. Now it is the soldiers' turn. They confer amongst themselves first to ensure that they all heard the same thing. You know, the translator being from a different Arabic country speaking a different dialect. And then there is likely to be a lively discussion between the translator and soldiers to clarify any misunderstanding and when the majority consensus is reached, they act on the instructor's command—*attack*.

This practice occurs not just in the military sector, but also in most public services such as medical and educational, which employ foreign contractors. Such contracts initially are with western countries that provide such services and training with complete technology transfer so that after a few years the local agencies can take over. It is this initial period of on-the-job training when funny things happen. What things? I'm glad you asked.

This should give you the flavor of it. During a highway auto accident emergency when the Canadian paramedics and their local trainee arrived at the scene, the trainee refused to leave his vehicle. When repeatedly asked why, he reluctantly answered that his boss had instructed him never to leave his vehicle unattended as it may be stolen. The frustrated Canadian paramedic, struggling to save the life of the accident victim, told the trainee in a stern voice to lock up his goddamn vehicle and attend to the emergency at once. Reluctantly, eventually he carefully locked up his vehicle and came out to help the Canadian. Would you believe it, while he assisted the Canadian the trainee managed to lose his car keys and yes, you guessed it, he was later told off by his boss. Finally, they managed to solve the problem by sending a driver with every trainee attending an emergency. See, when money is no object, solutions can easily be found. Well, almost always.

I remember a recent event. At an annual international powerboat-racing event a boat with a sudden surge of acceleration turned over at the starting point, spilling its driver into the shallow waters. One of the two high-powered rescue boats idling some distance away in the deep water, driven by the local macho drivers, rushed to the scene and in his zeal one of the rescue boat driver ran his monstrously powered boat right over the injured driver in the water, resulting in massive injuries to the already half-dead driver and severely damaging his own boat in the process as the propeller hit the sandy bottom. The second rescue boat driver refused to move since procedures call for both boats to be operational, allowing one boat to be always available as standby. The local paramedics decided to wait till a new boat arrived while the unconscious driver began to drown.

The Canadian paramedics weren't having any of it so they waded through the shallow waters and brought the unconscious driver to shore, placed him on a stretcher and started to give him emergency care. Thanks to the quick thinking of the Canadians, the driver survived. Right? Wrong. The local emergency physician, all 275 pounds of him, saw the foreign paramedics doing his job, got upset and came hurtling down the slippery boat landing area, shouting abuses and yelling at the Canadians to get away from his patient, and guess what? He tripped and fell. He landed right on top of the dying patient, rendering the poor man dead. Flat as a pancake. The patient broke the doctor's fall but couldn't prevent a few bruises and cuts. The local paramedics attended to the bruises and cuts on the doctor. It even made the headline in the local newspaper—*local doctor injured in a heroic attempt to save British powerboat driver*.

On the lighter side, halfway through the paramedics' training, an instructor from Canada was employed to give one month of special instructions to an extended class of trainees. When he finished, he was advised by the Director to repeat his course. When the instructor confronted the Director and asked why, the Director closed the door, offered the instructor lots of sweet tea and explained in a hushed tone that he had awarded a three-month catering contract to his cousin so the course must now be stretched to last three months.

No need to argue with the logic (or rather, the lack of it), just go with the flow and develop a sense of humor. And by the way, if you are traveling to this part of the world then a word of advice—get yourself the most expensive health plan that includes emergency evacuation away from here, far away to anywhere you don't have to deal with the local trainee paramedics. Just do it and thank me later.

30

AFTERSHAVE COCKTAIL

Something daring I like to do, when I am allowed by the one who controls my astrological stars, is to go to a party. You might think there is nothing daring about going to a party, but before you make that supposition take into consideration where I live. It is divinely magical in the strictly enforced non-drinking Arabian countries to have the chance to get sloshed. Perhaps because it's the taste of forbidden fruit, or is it just sheer stupidity that dares you to break the laws of the land? I would like to believe it is the former even though my wife thinks that it is stupid to go to such parties. Actually, she could be right in that going to such parties is okay but coming out of them is a stupidity. Confused? You won't be after you have finished reading this enlightening story.

First let me get this straight. Not all Arabian countries ban alcohol and there are degrees of freedom in the various Arabian countries about alcohol consumption. For example, countries such as Saudi Arabia, Iran, and Iraq strictly forbid alcoholic beverages. And it is in these countries that the expatriates tend to go overboard with their drinking. Now like I said before, going to such binge parties is technically okay since going in you have no alcohol in your bloodstream, but coming out of these parties in the wee hours of the morning is a different story altogether. If you are unfortunate enough to get caught drunk in such places then you are likely to get more than just a hangover. You are in for several days of imprisonment, lashing in public to cause more embarrassment than pain (though sometimes a severe lashing like 500 lashes or so can take the skin off your back—*no quality control*) and, finally, deportation to make you face the ultimate in horror—*the dreaded income tax*.

Many people come to work in these countries for an added bonus. They are here to dry out. But at the same time there are many expatriates who perhaps were never too keen on drinking alcohol in their own country and are drawn to illegal drinking parties in these strict Arabian countries by sheer stupidity…oops, I mean, the adventure.

You say how you could be caught drunk if they don't serve alcohol in theses strict Arabian countries. Well, I didn't say they don't have alcohol. It is just that you are not supposed to have alcohol. To be precise, there are two ways you can find yourself drunk. First, you could go to a non-Islamic embassy party where alcohol flows freely because embassy grounds are considered sovereign territories, something to do with a lame excuse like diplomatic immunity. If you attend diplomatic parties, make sure that you are driving a four-wheel drive with a full tank of gas. Why? Let me get back to that in a moment. I must admit I have never before seen people get drunk so quickly. The reason is that embassy parties last only a couple of hours (maybe because most ambassadors are old and like to go to bed early) and you are allowed to drink only while on the premises. So what do you do? Well, you do what every grown-up and sensible person does. You guzzle down liquor, any kind—beer, scotch, wine, vodka, or gin—by the liter and fast.

Now while you are drinking on the embassy grounds the only harm that could come to you is the self-inflicting damage you do to your own liver, otherwise, you are quite safe. But once you have decided to step outside while drunk then, obviously, you have taken the challenge a little too far.

Because the religious police who have nothing better to do than to protect you from the evils of alcohol are there to teach you a lesson—*remember the public lashing?* And the only recourse you may have to avoid the clutches of the religious police lurking in the neighborhood, bent on making an example out of you as an infidel, especially if drunk, is to avoid the roads. Shove your SUV into four-wheel drive and map your way home through the dark desert. Take my advice and get a GPS if you really want to be ahead on the power curve and make it home on a single tank of gas.

Did I say there were two ways to get drunk? I am losing my memory. I think it has to do with fast-paced ingestion of copious amounts of alcohol at too many embassy parties. Oh, I remember now. The second way, of course, is to make your own alcoholic drinks and host at-home parties. How does one find the ingredients to make alcoholic beverages in such strict countries? Ah, that's easy. You go to a local supermarket and head straight to that last aisle where it is a little bit dark and you will find on shelves and in the right order all the necessary ingredients—sugar, yeast and, of course, in glass bottles with air-tight pressure caps, cases of red and white grape juice.

You load up your cart with all these goodies and make your way to the line of cashiers, being sure to pick the one with a Filipino cashier. They are the experts—he will glance at the ingredients and if you have got it wrong, he will send you back to get more sugar or different yeast. If you are a new expat then make sure to pick up a five-gallon plastic drum or two and a siphon pump.

Now go home and fire your maid because you need her room to store your wine. Yes, in this land of black gold (oil to those who do not keep up with current affairs), one gets a house with maid's quarters. Mix all ingredients according to recipe (several available on the internet), and be adventurous, add your own personal touch. For example, I add a pot of tea per five-gallon drum to give it that extra tannic acid and flavor. A little bit of cinnamon is a treat. Yeah, let your imagination go wild. Now wait for a few months for the magic to happen and voila, you have your own poison and you can drink yourself silly.

A piece of advice, if you don't mind! Don't ever give splash-on aftershave as a Christmas present to your driver. I did that once and the poor sod thought it was an alcoholic drink so he drank it on his way home. At a police checkpoint he failed the

Breathalyzer test (the nose & sniff type) and, consequently, got thrown into prison where he called me, asking for help. I knew there was a good chance that the police may pay a visit to me at home the next day to question why my driver was drinking aftershave.

I had to make a painful decision—play innocent (with potentially horrible consequences) or destroy my stash of homemade wine. Well, I am not so fond of public lashings and even less of Canadian taxes. So, I worked all evening smashing every wine bottle in the kitchen sink, reducing each bottle to small pieces and putting it all in cardboard boxes. Later that night I took it all out to a remote part of the desert and buried it.

I waited nervously the next day and eventually, instead of the police, my driver showed up grinning from ear-to-ear. I looked at him questioningly, wondering how he'd managed to get out of prison, and he satisfied my curiosity by explaining that his uncle, who happened to know one of the prison guards, gave him a half-dozen bottles of a very fragrant aftershave in exchange for the release of his nephew. Okay, so don't give aftershave as present to your driver but if you do, make sure you too have an uncle, in case it is needed, who knows prison guards and of course has a few aftershave bottles to spare.

31

DRINK AT YOUR OWN PERIL

Complicated rules are the root cause of our drinking problems in the lenient Arab countries where serving alcohol is permitted in hotel bars. Why, you ask? Well, some of the drinking rules are confusing even when you are sober, and incomprehensible when you are drunk.

This is a true story as told to me by my friend. This friend who came to work in Arabia from Canada, a busy businessman always on the road, is married to a Russian lady. Russian? That is a story for another time. While he was traveling on one of his business trips, his Russian wife received guests from Germany and took them to a hotel bar for cocktails prior to dinner. A cocktail or two grew into three and four as they lapsed into a serious and rather loud discussion of how Russia and Germany are misunderstood by the rest of the world. They too were victims of the mayhem caused by Hitler.

Well, a stocky Polish lady sitting not too far away was not having any of this, so she grabbed her martini and approached the Russian table. She said in a cold and steely voice, "You Russians and Germans are not misunderstood by the Polish. We know you f--ked up our country."

Before she turned back to her table she poured her large martini over the head of the Russian lady. The response was swift. The Russian lady returned the favor. The heavy-set Polish lady lost her balance, fell and in the process, caught the edge of the table to cause a deep cut on her nose. The Polish woman called the police to press charges. A few minutes later police arrived and arrested the Russian on multiple charges of illegal drinking, causing a disturbance in a public place and inflicting bodily harm.

After a night in prison, the Russian was able to see her husband, who rushed back from his business trip. It was explained to him that the drinking of alcohol in this progressive city was only allowed at home and drinking in a public place is considered improper and might be (laws here are never well-defined and at times not even in writing) illegal.

"But you have bars in hotels here?" questioned the confused husband.

"Of course we do. They are for hotel residents," replied the policeman with a very stern voice and equally hard face and further added to make things quite clear, "you as a resident should only be drinking at home, or you should get a room in the hotel."

The husband finally understood that the local law (which was never publicized) allowed them to buy liquor (only after they paid for a permit) at designated stores, but they could drink only at home because it was not permissible for people to be on the street, in cars or in a taxi cab with any amount of alcohol in their bloodstream. So the residents could go to hotel restaurants for dinner but drinking alcohol was not legally allowed except if you wished to stay overnight at the hotel. After pleading ignorance and a lot of groveling on behalf of his wife, he was told to come back the next day to see the supervisor.

The next day he was told that his wife had already appeared in front of a judge, and was charged and sentenced to thirty days in prison. He was in shock but not as much as his wife was. He had to buy a bottle of sedatives for his wife and a bottle of scotch for himself—*to drink at home, of course*. The poor lady remained heavily sedated throughout her thirty days of imprisonment for doing something she didn't start and for breaking laws she hadn't known.

On the thirtieth day the husband with a large bouquet of red roses went to prison to receive his wife where he was informed that red roses weren't enough. He had to collect a release order for his wife from the court. Did anyone tell him about it before he showed up? Of course not. Another couple of days was spent rushing around from clerk to clerk in the various departments of the city court where he was finally told to go to the police station to get the relief letter.

While the wife waited another week over and above her thirty days' sentence, the police station promised her husband that they would soon send a fax to the prison asking them to release his wife. It did take them a few more days to get the fax system going but they, true to their word, did send a fax to the prison asking them to immediately release the Russian woman. Once the husband learned of it he quickly bought even a bigger bouquet of red roses and hurried to the prison gates. The poor woman had served now two weeks more than necessary and was desperate to go home. The prison supervisor had the fax on his table and when the husband arrived, he gave the fax to him, demanding, "We must get an original, fax is no good."

The flowers drooped. The husband stood there with his mouth open and jaw hanging down to the floor. The supervisor offered his empty vase for the flowers while the husband went again to the city police station to get the original release letter. Of course, with limited working hours, you cannot accomplish more than one task in a day. So, another day or two slipped by while the husband pleaded with the police officer in charge to give him the original release letter. A week later, all the necessary permission forms were gathered and the husband was issued the original release letter. *This surely will work*, the husband thought as he bought a colossal bouquet of pink roses for his wife. He was certain by now that red roses did not bring him luck. Armed with a bouquet in his left hand and the original letter in his right hand, he marched triumphantly into the prison supervisor's office.

By now the prison supervisor and the husband had developed the kind of friendship that comes from a lengthy relationship fraught with constant disappointments and sorrows. The supervisor offered the husband a comfortable seat, tea and biscuits, and broke the bad news in a low tone, "I am so sorry but I am bound by our procedures and policies."

"What on earth are you saying?" demanded the nervous husband as he started to do the mental math on how much the flowers had cost him thus far.

"They have misspelled your wife's name. It has to be correct for us to release her," the prison supervisor explained in an affable tone as he gradually slid his empty vase towards the husband. The husband wondered for a minute if the supervisor was a kinky man and this entire charade was for him to collect free roses but then he shook his head in disbelief, discarded the thought and rushed back to the police station to get a corrected, original release letter, which he knew by now would take a few days. While he waited for such a letter he replenished his wife's supply of sedatives.

Finally, four weeks after the expiration of the original four weeks' imprisonment, the Russian was allowed to go home. And would you believe it, the corrected release letter was sent by fax and as a result she was let go without waiting for her husband to collect her. Since the husband was not notified of this, the wife had to take a taxi home.

That night they drank themselves silly to forget the wretched experience and then went out for a walk to get some fresh air. While walking they were stopped by a policeman who suspected they were drunk in a public place—that is an offence, you know.

32

THE LEGEND OF A GOAT

This is a true story told to me by my friend Mohammed, who learned it from his friend Hussein, who in turn heard it from his cousin Abdullah. And I am sure Abdullah heard the story from a long line of other storytellers because the story is now a legend in the small town of Najran in the southwest of Saudi Arabia.

Now I know that passing through a chain of storytellers, the actual story may have gathered on its way to me a few interesting flavors, but what is important here is that the soul of the story is untouched, and truly reflects the evolution of modern life in this region's centuries-old tradition of simple living. Why am I so sure? Well, Mohammed assured me of the authenticity of this story and I for one believe him. And, my friend, if you had spent some time here like I have, you would believe him too.

Anyway, back to the story. The Bedouin are known for two traits—

hospitality towards strangers and a love for their animals, especially goats. Normally when a Bedouin is traveling with one of his four wives and his favorite goat in a pick-up truck, the goat sits in the passenger seat and the wives are outside in the back of the truck. Now, isn't that true love...for the animals, I mean? However, there are times (like with a new wife or a young wife) when an exception is made and the wife gets to sit inside the cab and the poor goat, in the back.

On one such exceptional and hot summer day in Najran, when this Bedouin was driving his Toyota pick-up with Habibi (the name of his goat that means darling) in the back of the truck and his new and number four wife (name neither known nor important to this story or otherwise) in the passenger seat next to him, he noticed a stranger walking on the hot and dusty road. He stopped and offered the stranger, who turned out to be an Egyptian, a ride in the back of his truck. The Egyptian hopped in next to Habibi and the truck continued its journey down the path. Soon the Bedouin spotted a scrawny Indian (an East Indian, you know, from India. This is not a cowboy story, so pay attention please.), walking barefoot so obviously he stopped again and the Indian gladly hopped in and joined the Egyptian and, of course, Habibi.

A few kilometers down the road the Egyptian tapped on the back window, the Bedouin stopped and the Egyptian disembarked and said farewell to Habibi and the Bedouin. Another five kilometers or so the Indian tapped on the back window and the truck stopped again. The Indian said farewell to the Bedouin and started to walk away with Habibi. This alarmed the Bedouin and he shouted, "Where are you taking my Habibi?"

"Not your Habibi anymore. I bought it from the Egyptian. He said it was his and I paid him good money for it," said the Indian in a polite but firm voice.

"But it isn't his to sell. The Habibi is my best friend, my family. Habibi was never .or sale. Please give her back to me," argued the Bedouin with an edge to his voice.

"I am sorry," reasoned the Indian, "but I gave away all the money I had. I need this goat to survive. You're the one with money and this truck. You go get the Egyptian and ask him to return my money and then you can have your goat back. After all, it is your fault because I met the Egyptian in your truck."

The Bedouin watched in horror as Habibi, the light of his life disappeared into the narrow dusty streets of a village with one end of a string around her neck and the other end firmly in the grasp of the Indian.

The Bedouin drove hurriedly to the nearest small town and reported the matter to the police station. Now, the police in this particular part of the country were very efficient and had their own methods for solving crimes. For example, if someone had committed a murder in a small village, the police would arrest everyone in the village and throw them all into prison until such time the villagers were ready to reveal which one had committed the crime. Boy, if nothing else, it teaches you to live in harmony at all times with the entire community of your village. Back to the story of poor Habibi. The police captain in charge took down the details and went on a search for the Egyptian and the Indian.

A house-to-house search gave no clue to the whereabouts of either of the two men or of Habibi, for that matter. They seemed to have disappeared into thin air. When the entire week went by with no results, the Bedouin became very depressed and often cried for his Habibi. Even his new and young bride was no match for the love of Habibi. With heart-wrenching pleadings from all the wives, the police agreed to take the Habibi case to the local ruler, who was considered the last word in any and all matters.

The ruler was moved by the sad story of the disappearance of Habibi and being himself an animal lover, ordered the police to make use of the newly acquired sketch artist, a very expensive resource acquired to assist in solving serious crimes, but hey, we are talking Habibi here. I guess the practice of throwing the whole village into jail to solve major crimes was losing popularity, so bringing in a sketch artist was their move towards modernization.

Without delay, the sketch artist got to work and soon all the mud walls of the village were covered with the artist's impression of Habibi. When the ruler saw this, he immediately summoned the police captain in charge and questioned him.

"You idiot, you were supposed to have developed the sketch of the Indian and not the goat he took away. You ask me all the time about getting new and expensive modern facilities to assist you and what do you do? You really are an embarrassment."

"But sir," pleaded the police captain, "the Bedouin says that all those Indians look alike but he's sure he could spot his Habibi from a mile away, and so could the villagers."

Rumor has it that Habibi was spotted in the next village by some villagers who had seen the posters. The ruler was a kind man so he gave the Indian palm dates, goat cheese and a few coins as incentive to return the goat back to the rightful owner. The Bedouin was delighted to get his Habibi back and also helped the Indian by giving him a job at his farm.

I hope they managed to catch the Egyptian too, you know for Habibi's sake.

33

KIDNAPPED IN YEMEN

The moment 'the one who commands respect' walked into my office I knew that look on her face, one that clearly expressed—*you are not adventurous enough*. Oh, yes. She has many expressions and I know them all.

"I want to go to Yemen to be kidnapped." Her voice was calm and she appeared composed. There was no visible sign of distress. As far as I could tell there had not been any catastrophic developments in our recent past causing her to make such a suicidal statement. My gaze narrowed in bewilderment but I didn't have to ask her anything as she volunteered, "Yemenis treat their kidnapped victims well, they give them the best house in the village, excellent food, and take them sightseeing. They never demand money and in exchange for their government providing a paved road or a schoolteacher or electricity, they let their kidnapped victims go unharmed."

Well, that sounds okay, I thought as I batted my eyelids, fighting the dizziness that had suddenly overcome me.

She continued, "They treat kidnapped victims as 'guests' and it is for a good cause, and it will be an adventure. I have booked two seats to go to Yemen next week."

Now this may sound a little strange, but it is the truth. Kidnapping foreigners is a way for poor Yemenis to pressure their government into meeting their simple demands. Maybe they have been watching too many Robin Hood movies. It is reported that many of the kidnapped tourists return carrying gifts from the kidnappers including silver jewelry and traditional daggers. A published account reported the experience of an Italian tourist who was held hostage for five days, saying it was a wonderful experience. Mr. Giorgio Bonanomi stated that the kidnappers fed him delicious lamb dishes and exotic fruits and he regretted that his country didn't have organized holidays like this.

I hurried to my Internet and conducted some research. This may interest you. During the period of six years from 1996 to 2001, there have been 157 kidnappings in Yemen. That is on average one tourist kidnapped every two weeks. Over seventy percent of these tourists were Italians, French, German and

British. You got to hand it to these Europeans. They sure know how to have a holiday on the cheap. There were only nine Americans and one Canadian. So, there was no way my wife was going to let Europeans get away with it, she was determined to increase the Canadian numbers.

Some people might tell you that kidnappers have killed their victims in Yemen. Yes, there were two such incidences, but it had to do with either the police shooting the hostages in confusion or the hostages attacking their captors in an unsuccessful attempt to flee. How ungrateful. The trick is to relax, enjoy and bring back some free gifts.

The following is more typical of what kidnappers do. A former Yemani army colonel kidnapped a Chinese accountant who was out for a stroll. The colonel demanded that the government cancel his retirement and give him back his army vehicle. He was simply bored and wanted to get back to work. What is wrong with that?

Here is another one. Two Italian women were kidnapped and the demand for a local voting station was made so that the villagers could vote for the local government election, they were simply frustrated by being ignored all those years.

Then there was the chairman of an Italian archaeological foundation who was kidnapped by a young tribesman who agreed to return him safely in exchange for employment in the military. Can you imagine how that would look on his record sheet: professional skill—*kidnapping*.

These kidnappers are daring people and proved it by kidnapping in broad daylight the Polish ambassador while he was visiting his dentist. I think the ambassador should have thanked his kidnapper for saving him from the Yemeni dentist's chair. Instead, the ambassador in protest went on a hunger strike and that made his captors very concerned for his health and they quickly returned him to his family. Such gentle souls.

The most interesting story is that of a French couple on their honeymoon who were kidnapped and the demand for a new school was relayed to the authorities. The government agreed and the tribesmen let the couple go. Later the same day the tribesmen found out that the government had alternative plans in case the couple was not released, they had intended to raid the village to free the honeymooners. This upset the kidnappers and they recaptured the couple. All they wanted this time was an apology from the government in exchange for the freedom of the French couple. When interviewed later the couple had indicated that they were having so much fun that they may extend their honeymoon in Yemen. That's the spirit. It is beside the point that upon their return to France the couple was examined by a professional psychoanalyst for choosing the destination of Yemen for their honeymoon.

The main targets of kidnapping are diplomats because they represent their respective governments, who might be in a position to put pressure on the Yemeni government to meet the captors' demands. Recently a diplomat and his wife were kidnapped and the captors demanded compensation for flood damage that occurred a few years ago. Trying to be smart, the husband told the captors that they were teachers and not diplomats. When the captors learned this they decided to free them for a good reason: teachers are poor and no government gives a hoot about teachers. However, before they could set them free a newsflash on TV reported the kidnapping of a diplomat couple in that area. This made the kidnappers mad and they increased their demand to include four tractors.

In 1999, a German midwife, her brother, their mother, her Yemeni husband and their three (Yemeni) children were kidnapped. The kidnappers quickly released the Yemeni husband and three children and made a few simple demands. Days went by and no word came. The kidnappers asked the German midwife to take a message to her husband. She left and never came back. The kidnappers felt hurt by this dishonest approach and asked for her to come back. No one responded and the angry kidnappers put her brother and parent in a truck and sent them back to their family, for they did not want anything to do with such a dishonorable family.

Perhaps the best story is about a Yemeni who was wanted for murdering a supermarket owner. The authorities kidnapped two of his brothers and asked him to surrender in exchange for the release of his brothers. This outraged the murderer and he did what he knew best, he kidnapped six tourists in order to obtain the release of his brothers. The authorities' plan backfired and they released his brothers.

Well, with all this excitement, who could resist such a grand vacation? Excuse me while I go and pack. Also, I need to learn in Arabic how to say, 'Please kidnap us, we are diplomats.' Wish me luck, and I hope we get kidnapped on the very first day because then the whole trip would be a real bargain.

34

ROMANCE IN YEMEN

Imust say I was nervous arriving in south Yemen for a ten-day holiday. Despite my wife's desire to be kidnapped in Yemen for a romantic adventure, I was more inclined to stay in a five-star hotel and enjoy a few out-of-city trips in a chauffeur-driven car.

While we were out for a day trip in a car provided to us by AVIS, our driver pointed out to us that we were on the highway famous for the largest number of kidnappings. My wife's face lit up and my jaw slackened. My wife adored the hospitality of Arabia and was convinced that Yemeni kidnapped tourists only to win simple favors from their government such as a paved road, a schoolteacher, or compensation for flood damage. And while they kept you as a hostage you were not only treated to delicious food, exotic fruits, and sightseeing, but you were also given gifts when you were set free.

It was like an 18-30 budget holiday with the exception that, instead of an age restriction of 18 to 30, it was more like the number of days you were expected to spend in captivity. The Yemeni government wasn't all that quick when it came to solving kidnapping cases.

I knew there was on average a kidnapping every two weeks in Yemen and here we were unwittingly increasing our chances to be kidnapped. I decided to change the subject and took an interest in our driver's background. He proudly stated that he was a Somali and came to this country when he was a teenager. When we asked what brought him to Yemen, he explained calmly that he had killed two soldiers in Somalia and it was no longer safe for him to live there. Great. Not only were we on a kidnapper's paradise highway, we were in the company of a self-confessed murderer.

Out on the deserted highway, our driver made a stop. We noticed that every few miles there was a person squatting by the highway selling bunches of green leaves. Yemen being so harsh and rugged in landscape, I had assumed that those tender, juicy-looking green leaves were for pet goats or possibly something you might boil to make a medicinal drink. Our driver stopped and bought a big bunch of green leaves that he laid carefully in his lap as he took off again at a breakneck speed. He began plucking leaves off twigs and once he had a handful, he popped them in his mouth. He repeated this process until his right cheek was all puffed up, filled with the magic green leaves.

Naturally I asked him about his strange behavior. He explained, "We call this quat and as you suck on these leaves for an hour or two, you feel quite high." While I was still absorbing the impact of the potential threat of kidnapping in the company of a self-confessed murderer, now I also had to factor in being driven at high speed on twisting, mountain roads by a lunatic who was getting high on some unknown narcotic.

The driver insisted that I give it a try. So as not to offend him, I popped a couple of leaves in my mouth and started to chew them very slowly. He passed me handful after handful that I pretended to put in my mouth, but instead I pocketed them. Later I discovered that at one time Yemen was a major grower and exporter of excellent coffee. But now most coffee plantations had been replaced by farms growing small, green-leafed plants that every Yemeni loved to suck on so as to fall asleep from late morning to later afternoon, a narcotic siesta.

We came to a small mountaintop village and my adventurous wife demanded we stop there for a walk. I thought it was a good idea too—to get some reprieve from a murderer high on natural drugs. While we strolled through the narrow streets we heard drums and then saw a wedding procession. Every man, and there were about fifty, had a Russian-made, rapid fire Kalashnikov machine gun looped over his shoulder.

As we stood pretending not to be there, the wedding celebration gathered intensity as indicated by fast-beating drums. Men were wielding their traditional knifes in the air in a mock fight, except now and then I spied a streaky red mark on people's arms. A few minutes later some of the men removed their rifles from their shoulders and started to shake them violently in the air and then the shooting began. They were deliriously happy and shooting everywhere in a haphazard way. Bullets were flying, zinging past our ears and ricocheting from the walls of nearby stone houses. Either they were very happy or were under the influence of those little green leaves—maybe both. Suddenly the bridegroom buckled and collapsed where he was standing, a flying bullet had hit him. We quietly backed up and departed hastily from the celebrations.

As we left the blood-soaked frenzy of a wedding celebration, we were heading to another mountain village where our driver wanted us to have lunch with a friend of his—another murderer from Somalia and a junkie? I wondered. He explained that his friend's was one of the most beautiful villages in Yemen and the government was trying to promote it as a tourist attraction. My wife was delighted with the offer. From the distance we could see the village, surrounded with gardens of beautiful blue and yellow flowers. Only when we got closer, we realized they were not flowers, but rather empty plastic bags thrown out by villagers as trash. I asked politely why the people wouldn't keep their beautiful and historic village clean, especially when they were trying to promote tourism. The response was an expression of deep thought and then a casual shrug of the shoulders.

We met his delightful friend who looked as if he was at least two pounds ahead of our driver in leaf chewing. He introduced us to his mother, who was the owner of the house and the cook. There were flies everywhere and an open sewer flowed freely by the side of the house. A cow was sitting in the courtyard, flicking flies with her tail.

The food was absolutely disgusting and not fit for human consumption. I put two sodden leaves into my mouth and for appearances (or out of fear that if I refused to take them then someone might shoot me), ate a few tiny morsels of whatever was in front of us. It looked like very raw pieces of flesh floating in watery curry and some dry bread pock-marked with holes with flies in them.

To make conversation, I asked the driver's friend why the government hadn't cleaned their village, the pride and joy of Yemen. He smiled and said that the villagers haven't had the time to put pressure on the government to provide proper sanitation for the village. Light dawned. What he meant was that the villagers were looking to kidnap a couple of tourists to create negotiating powers with the government. As I fainted I am sure I heard my wife shrieking with excitement.

35

HOW NOT TO DO BUSINESS IN ARABIA

The one thing that really gets to me is the almighty, know-it-all attitude of some of the executives back home. I once had a boss who bragged in our annual board of directors meeting that he knew everything there was to know about doing business in Arabia.

I remember once he asked me to take him to one of my clients from whom we were expecting a $350,000 engineering contract that eventually would have lead to $3.5 million in construction work. In a very cordial environment and over a cup of tea, my client asked for a price discount (customary everywhere in Arabia), to which my boss leaned back in his chair, stretched out his feet encased in pointy snake-leather cowboy boots on my client's desk and said, "Partner, I can do anything. If you sign right now, I will give you a price of $250,000. What do you say to that?"

My client tried to whisper something to me in Arabic. My boss interrupted him and continued, "You don't know what to say now, do you? You didn't expect me to give you such a sweetheart of a deal. That is okay, partner, we will teach you the tricks of the trade, just stick with us. Sign the contract."

I explained in a low voice to my boss that the Arab client found him offensive and rude (especially for showing the soles of his shoes to him, considered a great insult in this part of the world), and had asked for us to leave before he called for security. Later, and in front of my president, my boss blamed me for losing that contract and for not having a closer relationship with the client.

On another occasion the same boss over a luncheon meeting with an Arab client demanded, "Say, why don't you guys eat pork? It is a mighty fine product. Better than this scrawny goat stuff you folks brag about."

The client smiled politely and asked to be excused to go to the washroom and never came back. When I later explained to my boss that bringing up talk about eating pork with Arabs is a big no-no, he dismissed my statement with a sweeping hand gesture and said, "Nah, that guy was just nervous about having lunch with a senior executive."

Now I could understand if my boss was a part owner of the firm or had an influential daddy, but as far as I could tell he was hired for his marketing and sales skills. The reason it is hard for me to fathom this is because in every meeting he attended with me we ended up losing sales. He was a walking self-help manual on how not to sell.

Once a year and every year there is a major trade show for the engineering and construction industry in Tehran and, under the banner of our Canadian subsidiary of the US company, we decided to participate and set up a booth. My boss insisted that the booth must have two pretty girls because that is what sells engineering and construction services. I explained, unsuccessfully I might add, to my boss that it may work in the US but it wouldn't work in Iran. To which my boss posed a very diplomatic question: Did I want to keep my job or not?

Since my boss had an Irish-American background and an Irish passport, we managed to get him to visit us during the trade show. When he arrived at the booth and was greeted by two women dressed in a local black dress (Abaya) covering them completely from head to foot, he demanded to know why we didn't hire pretty girls.

I explained that they were very pretty, but in public places you could not see their faces or any part of their body. Also, they were not allowed to speak to strangers. To my amazement he laughed and said, "Well, it is kind of cute...intriguing like. You know, a bit of a mystery. I like it. Carry on, boys. And listen," he whispered in my ear, "maybe the ladies want to have a drink with me in private this evening."

Mystery, I laughed. What he didn't know was that we had hired two (very slim) construction men to pose as mysterious women. The next day we explained to him that ladies were not allowed by their parents to visit him—*strict parents*, we told him. He just shook his head and muttered something about their misfortune.

At a gala dinner the next evening, he boasted to the Iranian Minister of Industry how he helped out the local economy by providing employment to two local girls. At about midnight that night my boss was escorted by special police to the airport and deported back to the States. His passport was blacklisted, denying him any future entry into the country.

The best incident happened in Saudi Arabia where my boss in his usual charming way challenged a senior executive of the

Ministry of Industry by stating that the locals needed to revolt against the ruling family. The world needs an American way of living, Texas style. To his horror he was ejected from the meeting room by the local police, arrested and sent to prison.

Visiting him in Saudi prison was one of my most satisfying moments. He asked me if he had said something or done something wrong. I assured him that he was a brave man and who knows, his earlier talk may have sown the seeds of a future popular uprising. He asked me how long would that take. I felt like hitting my head on a brick wall. No, I tell a lie. I felt like hitting his head on a brick wall. Maybe that would have redistributed some of his grey matter, allowing him to start thinking in a logical fashion.

Well, after several phone calls and promises and written assurances, we managed to get him out of prison. Funny, it took three days to get him out of there. The Saudi authorities blacklisted him and gave him a week's notice to leave the country and told his employer to make sure he never came back.

No sooner was he out of prison than he contacted the American embassy and threatened to sue the Saudi royal family for his unlawful arrest. The embassy blacklisted him and made sure he was on a plane with a one-way ticket to Texas. That has got to be one of my happiest days.

The moral of the story is that if you are a Texan firm and want to be successful in the Arabian engineering and construction industry, don't hire Irish-Americans who claim to know everything about business in Arabia. Trust me, they don't, especially if they are in the habit of wearing snake-leather cowboy boots.

36

GUESS WHAT'S FOR DINNER?

When I arrived in Saudi Arabia I was told that to have tea with an Arab colleague was a sign of acceptance of you as an expatriate in their country. Well, I wanted to be accepted so I switched from coffee to tea and before you know it, I was drinking gallons of tea every day. I became so well accepted that I received an invitation from Mohammed, an Arab friend of mine, to a dinner party at his home. This is supposed to be a rare honor.

Mohammed gave me directions to his house that looked more like a pirate map of hidden treasure. There were camels and car wrecks sketched on the map as landmarks. Mohammed explained that it was today's map as the camels shown on the map had arrived only the previous evening and were expected to be there for a day or two.

The dinner invitation was for seven o'clock and I set off from my house at three p.m. Although the house was only about fifteen kilometers away, I didn't want to be late. Besides, I wanted to make sure that the camels drawn on my map were still there and hadn't wandered off. As I drove around in my friend's district, I realized that a lot more camels must have arrived than were on the map. Later it was explained to me that I should have looked for camels that were standing up as illustrated on the map. The camels that arrived later would have been tired from their journey and therefore must be sitting down resting. How silly of me, I should have thought of that. I noted that for future reference. Also, I decided to brush up my map-reading abilities.

So I was late but only by fifteen minutes. The rest of the guests didn't start arriving until nine p.m. Another note I made for future reference, always add two to three hours to the time of an invitation.

My friend's house was more like a small palace. Like all the other houses nearby, it too was surrounded by a high, perimeter wall with a guard at the front gate. Inside, it was a huge house divided into several rooms and corridors. I was looking forward to having a little chat with Mrs.

Mohammed to personally say thank you for the dinner invitation. To be honest with you, I wanted to talk to a Saudi woman, since at my place of employment we were all men and I had never had an opportunity to talk to a Saudi woman.

But no such luck. It was explained to me that women in Saudi do not socialize with men. I wasn't even offered a tour of the house as women were present there and that meant the men must stay in the quarters that were specifically designated for men only. The women of the house were not allowed to venture where men entertained and vice versa. As I pondered this issue, I thought: *What a great idea. We should do this in Canada. A party where sports chat, cigars and beer could flow without any gossip on hairstyles, shoe designs and the color of nail polish.*

Anyway, the first three hours saw tea in ceremony after tea ceremony being served. All sorts of Mohammed's friends and family members kept arriving and finally the crowd in the living room swelled to about fifteen men.

As midnight approached, hunger cramps in my stomach intensified. I began to wonder if I heard Mohammed right that this was supposed to be a dinner. But I didn't need to panic. To my great relief dinner arrived soon after midnight. Everyone sat on the floor in a large circle and extraordinarily large serving dishes were placed in the center of the circle. They contained tons of saffron rice, whole roasted lamb, grilled chickens and something else that looked like a goat's head…yes, it was, and I gazed at it nervously.

Everyone grabbed and tore a piece of lamb or pulled a large chunk of grilled chicken and scooped rice with their cupped hands. Mohammed asked me if he could serve me some meat. I said yes. Not a good decision. Mohammed, who was sitting closer to the roast lamb dish and about four men away from me, leaned forward and tore off a large piece of lamb then tossed it towards me. Miraculously it landed in my plate. Mohammed scooped some rice and asked if I would like some and I vigorously shook my head in the negative.

In less than twenty minutes the place looked like a battlefield. Pieces of meat and chicken and splattering of rice were everywhere. Funny, I thought, no one had touched the goat's head. It must have been placed there for decoration purposes. Wrong again. Mohammed leaned over once more and this time he plucked out the eyes from the goat's head, walked over to where I was sitting, and placed them in my hand. On my open palm, I saw two sad-looking goat's eyeballs staring right at me. Mohammed explained that I was the guest of honor and it was his pleasure to serve his chief guest with the goat's eyes that I must chew, for they were delicious. The other guests smacked their lips and looked at me with envy, mm…yummy…eyeballs. My mind was struggling to come up with any excuse that would save me from this daunting task, however, I had no choice but to place the boiled eyeballs in my mouth, I could not be discourteous to my gracious host.

They were soft and chewy at the same time…with not much taste. Just like any boiled eyeballs would taste, really. Everyone cheered and then they all stood up and went to a sink that was plumbed right in the living room to wash their hands. The washbasin was covered with rose petals and rose-scented water was poured on their hands to clean and refresh them. I wanted to drink the rose-scented water to get rid of the awful feeling in my mouth that was left behind by chewing the eyeballs. I felt uncomfortable thinking that there were two eyes looking at my insides...the poor goat.

After dinner, you guessed it, more tea. I drank copious amounts of tea and in big gulps to ensure that the eyeballs would remain in my stomach and, hopefully, digest quickly. Two hours after midnight the dinner finally came to an end and one by one all the friends and family members bid their host goodnight. Their gracious smiles and warm handshakes humbled me. When I got home I went for a long walk, I thought it might help expedite digestion, as I didn't want those eyeballs to roll around in my stomach all night.

I must say my desire to be accepted in Arabic society through dinner invitations died after that first experience. I am now very happy as an antisocial person at my workplace and have switched back to coffee.

37

SELECTIVE MEMORY

I have no idea how I survived for so many years in the sales and marketing profession with my disability. You see, I cannot remember names and faces. Now this is like offering the job of a Formula One racing driver to a person who doesn't know how to drive, or one suffering from a fear of water aiming to join the Navy Seals.

I would visit a client company and the person I was meeting would suggest that I meet with his boss. We would walk into his boss's office and he would greet me with a big smile and say, "Hey, how are you? I haven't seen you since we had lunch together last month." At this point my mind would be searching every database in my memory bank trying to figure out who the heck this man was. Worse still is when some friend bumps into me on the street and stuffs a ten dollar bill in my hand, thanking me for bailing him out of a tight situation a day or two ago. Forget the damn ten-dollar bill, I can't even remember who the hell this friend is.

It is not that my mind would go blank at a meeting, it seems that it is already blank. What I mean is that my mind has an uncanny ability to purge the memory of most names and recognition of faces minutes after I meet people. And remember, I am in sales.

Mind you, this does offer a bright spot or two. At dance parties I usually get more dances than others with strange girls simply because I cannot remember if I already asked them for a dance or not, so I ask again and again. Poor ladies, they think I am persistent in my approach and they usually give into my second, third or fourth request for a dance. Lately this has backfired as recently at a busy dance party some irritable lady made quite a fuss, asking which part of NO I didn't understand—*I don't go dancing anymore.*

My wife knows about this condition of mine and God bless her, she is sympathetic. If we agree to meet at a restaurant during my lunch break, she will call me before lunch to say that she will be the one with a red rose between her teeth. You may laugh at that, but she is dead serious. I think she does it to stop me flirting with other women under the pretense that I didn't know to whom I was talking, so there goes the upside, if there ever was one, to my peculiar condition.

You know how it is on certain days when you wake up more tired than when you went to bed and look in the bathroom mirror only to find it hard to focus on your reflection through narrowly opened eyes. Well, I have a different problem altogether on those days—I have a hard time remembering who the hell that strange-looking guy in the mirror is. You see I forget my own face.

So, I decided to learn a few tricks to remember names and faces. Once I saw this man on TV who would meet with the audience as they arrived at his show (about 100 people), and after they took their seats, people at random would stand up and he would roll out their names without hesitation. To me this was nothing less than magic. The host explained it was all due to memory tags, when someone says his name you observe his face and attach something special about that person's facial features, dress style, or body appearance to his name. For example, Tom could be a 'fat' person, Jim could be 'pointy ears,' Ann could be 'thunder thighs,' and so on and so forth. These memory tags trigger the associated name when you see a person.

Right? Wrong. It may work in the western world but in Arabia it was as useful as a size-eight shoe person winning a brand new pair of size ten shoes. Confused? You won't be when I tell you that the entire race of Arabian people in this region somehow manage to look like an army of clones. Just about all of them wear similar if not almost identical loose-fitting, large over-shirts, called 'Thobes.' To further complicate matters, they are almost always white in color and they cover the entire body from the neck down. Ah ha, you say. What about their hair and facial features? Sorry, not much luck there either. They all wear identical-looking headdresses that have a large piece of cloth that hides the top of the head, its sides and over half of the face.

So during my initial years in Arabia, I tried to call everyone sir, including my tea boy (at this point you office professionals in Canada should be feeling jealous of us in Arabia having tea boys who throughout the day take care of our tea and coffee needs with a smile and their head bowed), to avoid any potentially embarrassing situations. This was okay for a while in an office environment, but then friends started to complain about my formal behavior. I was getting desperate and finally sought help from my lady wife, since she is a doctor and good at helping people out, you know Florence Nightingale and all that. As a true professional, she advised me to go see a professional. I think doctors are paranoid about malpractice liabilities, don't you? But she did give me a great tip. She explained that in her emergency clinic, doctors see about 500 patients a day every day and the majority of the male patients are either called Mohammed or Abdullah.

So there you have it. All I had to do was address my local colleagues either as Mohammed or Abdullah and I would have a one in two chance of getting it right. I think when I finish working in Arabia I am going to work in Korea where I understand eight out of ten males are called Lee…how can I lose?

Oops. I'd better run because she, what's her name, is shouting that dinner is on the table.

38

PROFESSIONAL ENGINEER

Now here is something I can say with some certainty. If you are an engineer (like me), you will like this story and if you aren't, then you will love it. The reason being that engineers have to analyze everything before they accept it as valid and, of course, it takes time to analyze things properly, by which time you won't see much humor in anything. You see subtle humor is all about timing.

When I decided to work for a large, internationally acclaimed and state-owned energy company in one of the Arabian countries, the name of which shall be withheld (for reasons obvious to the world and not so obvious to CNN), I decided to gain from the experience of one of the world's fastest growing corporations. From day one there was severe discontent amongst the eighteen local engineers who worked in my department. They did not like the company offering me the position of Director because I was a foreigner and hadn't lived in their country as long as they had. Besides, they thought it was inappropriate to ask a person to lead that was, how they put it, not the son of the land. Well, it all makes sense to me. My twenty-three years of management and international experience compared to their average three-to-five years of local experience, of course, had no relevance—*politics first, business afterwards*.

This situation, to my utter amazement, was solved by the senior management of this huge supposedly bureaucratic organization with swift action, giving all eighteen local engineers the title of director without any change in their responsibilities, and changing my job title to Vice President. As you can guess, the solution was short-lived in its success but fear not, management was not about to be disturbed by these new complaints and got it right this time by making all of us Vice Presidents.

Mohsen was my favorite. He lived in a time warp. He would always ask a question immediately after an answer to the problem was given. His timing was impacable. For example, when I would finish explaining a subject and conclude by saying something to the effect of "…and that is how you calculate return on investment," Mohsen would immediately raise his hand and ask, "That is interesting, but how do you calculate return on investment?"

At this juncture you would wonder if he were serious or just sleepy, or more likely, seriously sleepy. But it was hard to decipher this from his facial expression, as his eyes were set close to the bridge of his nose with an overhang of narrowing furry eyebrows, always looking intently at me. Even more amusing was when he would offer an answer to a question that he had asked himself about fifteen minutes ago.

Another consideration. Time management in Arabia has two specific problems—*time and management*. Time has no value here and, of course, there is no point in managing something that is worthless. Those who are born with a silver spoon in their mouth, liberally coated with crude oil (sorry, black gold), don't seem to have any incentive to learn management skills. After all, if they can afford to pay us (rather well I must admit and tax-free to boot) to manage their affairs, then why should they bother to even get up in the morning? Ah ha, but how would they know that strange pilgrims like us who are here to create our own tax-free wealth are not deploying Enron-type practices for our own good. So one day, a very rich-looking and connected (to the powers that control more than just business) local staff member approached me and demanded that I teach him everything I know about management skills. I looked at his heavy gold Rolex, diamond cufflinks and a set of Rolls Royce keys that he was playing with and said, "Sure, Abdullah, and how many years have you been given by your superiors to accomplish this?"

He glanced casually at his Rolex and said, "By four this afternoon, okay?"

There was an awkward silence between us as I tried to gather my thoughts to say something nice (to protect my neck) with an undertone of sarcasm (to satisfy my soul). Abdullah noticed my discomfort and pursed his lips as he uttered, "But I am a reasonable man. If that is too soon then let us say by noon tomorrow?"

My lower lip started to quiver with a nervous twitch as the need for the satisfaction of my soul started to take precedence over saving my neck. I had this acute desire to express myself, as my teenage son with a bright blue streak in his black hair would say, when Abdullah closed the discussion by commanding, "And no later than noon because tomorrow afternoon I have to fly out to go visit my mother in Marbella on my yacht."

It gets easier with time when you begin to understand that you will always be a lowly engineer, with decades of international management experience or not, and they will always be the rich oil sheikhs. One simply has to keep one's head down and curb any desire ever to shake a sheikh. So, I created several four-inch sleek black binders with hundreds of photocopied pages from Harvard Business Review magazines, adorned them with the personal name of my student (sorry, I mean my rich sheikh friend) for him to demonstrate to the world that he was uniquely qualified by possessing this personal dossier of the best management skills information, and as a result I never had to teach him anything or interfere with his visit to his mother. I shouldn't mention the gift of an expensive watch I received from him as a token of appreciation for meeting his schedule.

As my collection of watches and influence grew, created by my superior teaching methods to impart management skills to the local sheikhs who were born to antagonize the world with their oil wealth, I was rewarded with the responsibility of developing a $100-million R&D center for the Corporation. All they wanted was a world-class or, in other words, an expensive R&D center that would impress the world with their wealth. An Iraqi advisor (yes, they have a variety of them) advised some of the decision-makers that the best industrial inventions, such as the formula for the benzene ring structure, were conceived in dreams. That was enough. The Company instructed me to build a small hotel within the R&D complex for the local scientists to be able to sleep after lunch so they could dream up new inventions. You might think I am joking. I thought that too and paid no attention to their request and as a result my bonus on the inauguration of the new hotel-less R&D center was my pink slip.

Anyone need a Middle East-experienced engineer?

39

THE DAY AT A CONFERENCE

Did you know what the true definition of a consultant is? A consultant looks at your watch and tells you what the time is. See, when you have money to burn, you do foolhardy things like asking consultants to tell you what you already know. I should know this well because I am one of them. No, not the guy with the money to burn (I wish I was though…sigh), get it right, I am a consultant.

Well, if there is a job category that could top that of consultant, then that is the conference organizer. Get a load of this. In Arabia, conference organizers typically charge about $2000 per participant and you can bet your bottom dollar there will be at least 300 suckers who will attend. Why? Simple, you can expense it. The big bad corporations may negotiate your salary down to dollars and cents based on your skills, expertise, past performance, references and some international grading system, but when it comes to attending some silly conference at a resort location costing thousands, no problem, they will send you there in the name of networking and market intelligence. Mind you, I am not complaining, simply stating the facts.

Now $2000 is just the attendance fee and all it gets you is a book of conference proceedings and two buffet lunches for a two-day conference. You can do the math, but I figure that such an organization cleans out at least $600,000 in revenue and about $500,000 in net profits. That is per conference, my friend, and I have seen attendance as high as 1,000 or even more in some of these conferences.

No matter how unpromising a conference is, people still flock to each in the hundreds and for one reason, it is a perk. I do believe that people would work harder if they could get a decent raise rather than attendance at some silly conference. Don't believe it? Try this. Ask a white-collar employee if he or she would like to go on a couple of all-expense paid conferences (that would cost the company about $10,000) or would rather like a cool $10,000 in their pocket. Right? Right.

Anyway, last week I was at a conference and get this. A Singapore firm had organized the conference, it was held in Dubai in the United Arab Emirates, and British experts who were of Indian origin were invited to talk about opportunities in the Middle East. Confused? You won't be when I explain the quality or rather the lack of it at such a conference. Mind you, there was something at this conference that was available in abundance—humor. Let me explain. Other than Indian-born British experts, there was a funny mix of all sorts of experts from Libya, Yemen, Sudan, Jordan, Saudi Arabia and Kuwait who were making presentations.

My favorite at this conference was the speaker from Yemen. He approached the podium and his opening remark was, "This first time I speak, I not speak in public in Yemen, too many people, confusion coming."

Now to make matter worse, the tiny microphone in the shape of a small pearl or a rose bud was attached to the podium by a flexi stem that obviously had seen better days. Periodically the microphone flexi stem would droop under its own weight and the Bangladeshi technician was quick to run to the podium and straighten it so the audience could hear the speaker again. The poor

Yemeni speaker was also nervous for another reason. He was asked by his government to give a presentation on the modernization of an obsolete 7,000 barrels per day refinery and ask for financial help from international investors. This was hard and embarrassing, as speakers from Kuwait and Saudi Arabia had just finished giving their presentation on self-funded, brand new projects of billions of dollars worth, 400,000 barrels per day refineries.

Nervousness made the Yemeni fidgety and he started to shake and often banged his head on the microphone as he leaned forward to look at the laptop for presentation slides. With one such untimely move, he lurched forward too quickly while still speaking and at the same time the flexi stem drooped and he swallowed the tiny microphone still attached to the flexi stem. The microphone, stuck in the back of his throat, started to choke him. The Yemeni began to make horrible choking noises amplified, of course, by million watt amplifiers. The whole auditorium began to sound like a horror movie soundtrack. The Bangladeshi couldn't take it anymore and rushed to help him and in the process knocked the Yemeni flat on his back on the ground while the microphone wire attached to the podium brought the whole podium crashing down on top of the Yemeni.

Well, the Yemeni survived and was even able to finish his talk. In his halting English, he concluded with the remark, "We all good people with our own AK 47s, we protect you, please come and invest. We give many incentives to you. Good scenery, good mountains, good rifles. Come. Come."

But this wasn't the end of it. At the conclusion of all the presentations, during the question-and-answer session, anytime someone asked the Yemeni a question he would simply say, "No understand, no answer." When the Yemeni offered the same answer the third time, the chairman of the session whispered in his ear something to the effect that he must answer. He understood that and offered an explanation, "I'm sorry. My office in Yemen is in refinery, it's too noisy. I am almost deaf. Can't hear what you say."

This brought the house down. A participant yelled in the hand-held microphone, "Why do you work in a refinery? Do you like it?"

"I was the minister of customs before," he explained hesitantly, "my president, he say I choose to either become a diplomat or chief of national refinery. I don't like wearing suits so no point being a diplomat. So, I am in refinery."

And I, or rather my company, paid two thousand dollars plus expenses for this. Well, they are the pillars of our economy, or maybe they just need excuses for tax write-offs. Oh, I must be quiet. The Iranian speaker is about to start the afternoon session.

"Welcome. We are all brothers here, fellow refiners, except, of course, if you are from the land of the devil, America...." Political? Nah. He was simply humoring the crowd. Of course, I felt like moving close to the Yemeni, hoping he was carrying his AK47 for protection.

40

SMELLING LIKE A ROSE

Planning a routine business meeting in Arabia requires you to have nerves of steel, a sense of humor, an alternative employment strategy and an updated life insurance policy. Don't believe me? Okay, let me share with you an account of my recent business day when I had planned to meet at 9:30 a.m. the Vice President of a large refinery. Simple? Anything but.

First of all, the meeting was in a neighboring country, but that was not the problem. I'd bought a ticket on the previous day and went to the airport to board my flight. "Where is your visa?" they asked. I explained that my travel agent had told me that I didn't need a visa as I hold a Canadian passport. "True," they said, "but only if you travel on a certain airline like the airline of the destination country." I went back to my travel agent and he cancelled and reissued a new ticket on the required airline. Back to the airport and wait for four hours to catch the right airline.

A forty-five minute flight brought me to my destination. So why not drive, you ask. Are you kidding? Driving across the border requires several days of securing a variety of permits and a different type of visa. So, I arrived at the destination airport. My local and Arab business development manager, who is really my driver with a branch office car, was there to receive me and take me to my hotel for the next morning's meeting. I instructed my manager to pick me up at 8:00 a.m. since the drive to the refinery was about 45 minutes and I didn't want to be late. My manager cum driver advised me that meeting with such high position people demanded that we must not be late and might even show up early, so to avoid any unforeseen delays, he promised to pick me up at 7:45 a.m. I liked his foresight, a rare commodity in this part of the world.

After some Arabic food and local champagne made from fruit juices and Seven-up at the hotel's Paris Café, I went up to my room. All night long I tossed and turned as I lay in my bed in the only American hotel, with tanks and machine guns posted at the hotel gate for the guests' security. Finally, dawn broke and after a long shower, I went down to the Paris Café for a couple of cups of strong Arabic coffee. At 7:45 I stood on the porch (a few feet away from a military tank) with no sign of my driver, so I called him up on his mobile. He was asleep. At 8:15 he turned up unwashed with eyes still half-closed.

"Why didn't you call me earlier?" he demanded in a frustrated voice and added, "Now we're going to be late and it is such an important meeting." He mumbled something inaudible after that and I was pleased that I could not hear it. The day had already started badly and I didn't want it to get any worse.

"But, Abdullah," I said as I looked at him with a surprised look on my face, "we had agreed last night we'd leave at 7:45 a.m. You suggested it. Remember?" Well, that was enough to upset him. He took off like a rocket in his small Mitsubishi Lancer that was at least 15 years old and not fit to travel at a speed of 150 km and hour. I struggled to put my seatbelt on, as I could only find one end. He told me to hold it across my chest.

"Where is the company car?"

"My brother took it last night for an important party. He promised to bring it back this morning but he might still be sleeping," he explained casually.

"No kidding," is all I could say. Abdullah made one stop at a local garage to pick up a packet of cigarettes and a large cup of very black and thick coffee. Now here we are with sleepy Abdullah driving at 150 km an hour, holding a burning cigarette in his left hand and a large cup of hot coffee filled almost to the brim in his right hand and oh, yeah, no seatbelts. With the wind rushing in through the open windows, messing up my otherwise neatly groomed hair (I have only a few hairs that I arrange one by one), I sat there squinting my eyes and holding my seatbelt across my chest.

I tried to keep Abdullah calm by giving him the philosophical gems of my Buddhist teachings. I explained to him that life is too short to worry about meetings, and there are other things in life, such as family and children, that are far more important. But to be on the safe side, I called up the VP's office and advised them of our unfortunate delay. At 9:15 we rolled in. Then Abdullah did something inexplicable. From the glove compartment he took out a large spray bottle, pointed it towards my chest and gave a couple of squirts of rose perfume, saying, "Very important meeting, you must smell nice."

Together we walked into the conference room, wearing a rose garden on my chest and a large stain on the front of my white shirt, to meet with a very upset Vice President. He suggested or rather demanded straightaway that we do some free-of-charge engineering studies for his refinery. As I nodded my acceptance, or rather submission in the form of an apology for being late, he mellowed out a bit and from a side table, picked up a small spray bottle and gestured to offer some perfume. Instinctively I put both hands up and stuttered, "No, no, I'm trying to give it up."

The meeting lasted two hours as I continued to choke on my own perfume and the Vice President enlightened us with his accomplishments and explained to us various trophies that were on display in the meeting room that he had received as the most valuable management person. After several cups of dark and strong Arabic coffee and numerous chocolates, we were back on the highway. That is all I wanted—Abdullah high on nicotine and sugar. I felt like dousing him with the remainder of the rose spray. As he sped down the highway close to 200 km an hour, scratching his unwashed body and mumbling something about how he always wanted to be a rally driver, I was busy praying to my God and his, too, to grant me safety and grant Abdullah sanity.

To salvage the day, I made a few phone calls and set up a meeting with another client late in the afternoon in the industrial park about eighty kilometers away. First we decided to go to a café, the only café in the industrial park, for lunch. Walking into the café I knew instantly I had made a big mistake. There were about four or five tables occupied by heavy-set Afghans (presumably long-distance lorry drivers or Taliban—*both extremely dangerous*) with long black beards and checkered headdresses looking like Al Qaeda terrorists or prime candidates for wannabe suicide bombers, the image we are so familiar with thanks to CNN. Their bloodshot eyes examined me from head to foot as I walked in with my red tie and black silk suit.

The Egyptian café owner shook his head in disapproval and reluctantly unfolded a rusted tin table and two rickety old chairs in a dimly lit corner and I let Abdullah order our food. One large Afghan walked up to our table, touched my bright-red tie and asked if I was thinking of committing suicide. I smiled nervously and wondered if he actually had a sense of humor or perhaps was offering his assistance. Abdullah came to my defense and told the Afghan I was not an American but a Buddhist. After a long stare the Afghan walked back to his table and ploughed into his large plate of red and yellow rice.

I hunched over the table pretending to tie an undone shoelace under the table but in actuality undoing my tie knot and then I slowly removed my tie and stuffed it in my sock. Better to be safe than be hanged, I say. I noticed everyone was now watching TV and the breaking news was—suicide car bomb killing Lebanon's most famous man, Rafik Hariri. The wannabe terrorists looked in my direction, pointed their stocky thick fingers at me and said, "CIA." You realize that in this part of the world all the bad things, from assassinations to earthquakes, are blamed on the CIA. Who knows, maybe they are right. I quickly ate some of my mountain of rice and left the café in a hurry to wait in the car for Abdullah. My phone rang and the second meeting was cancelled.

The following week when Abdullah came to visit me in Bahrain, he explained that he really liked me and wanted to offer his help to save me from my sinful life of drinking wine and watching MTV. To save my soul he would help me convert to Islam, he explained as he slowly sipped on beer. I looked at him questioningly and he grinned and was quick to offer an explanation, "Oh, I will get lots of points for saving you by converting you to Islam, so I can afford to drink beer." Go figure.

If you'll excuse me, I need to plan my next week meetings while my business development manager, driver and savior is here. "Hey Abdullah, have another beer."

41

THE FINAL CURTAIN

Traveling by air is no longer my preferred mode of transportation, but then I am stuck with it, for there aren't many good alternatives to crossing the Atlantic. Oh, I know, you will say that people have tried rowing and sailing across it, but trust me when I tell you that the food and drink services suck on such alternatives. Besides, you can't trust their schedules.

Over the years I have been subjected to many flying misadventures but none like when I was asked to fly from Riyadh to Houston to attend a conference. I always prefer a window seat so I can sleep undisturbed during long-haul flights. Upon boarding, I found a local sitting in my pre-assigned window seat. I politely explained to him his mistake and he, with a casual gesture of his hand, told me to sit somewhere else. Now a little irate, I complained to a very pretty but nervous Filipina airhostess. She whispered, "I'm sorry, sir, but it is their country and on Saudi Airline they can sit wherever they like. Please take another seat."

I wasn't satisfied with her answer so again confronted the gentleman occupying my seat and this time he obliged me with an explanation that obviously suited him. "First come, first serve. Next time, don't be late."

Grudgingly, I took another seat. As the non-stop, direct Saudi Airline jet took off from Riyadh, I made myself comfortable in my spacious business-class seat. A few minutes later the seatbelt sign went off and the occupier of my seat went to the washroom. That gave me the opportunity I'd wanted. I moved his belongings to my seat and took possession of my pre-assigned seat. Upon his return from the washroom, he threw a fit and I very humbly gave him my explanation, "Finder's keepers. Next time, cross your legs." And that is what I did to keep my seat all the way for several hours to New York. From there, I took a connecting flight to Houston, but not before I rushed to the bathroom and let out the biggest sigh that sounded more like a shriek of utter joy.

This journey was just a preamble to what was about to come. Upon my return journey I was given a rather circuitous routing: Houston to San Diego to New York to London to Riyadh. Why? That is what I would like to know, too. Maybe it has something to do with human interference of local travel experts with computers.

The flight from Houston took off in an oncoming hurricane. Ascending through a curtain of thick, dark clouds, the plane shook like a matchbox and I prayed, promising that if I survived this I would never travel by air again—*rowing across Atlantic was not a bad option*. Survive we did and I did manage to reach San Diego for an overnight stay. That night one of the most severe earthquakes ever to hit San Francisco occurred. The guy on CNN said that they had been expecting a long-overdue major earthquake, but this wasn't it, although their experts postulated that a big one might hit San Diego that night.

I thanked CNN for the heads up and spent the night wandering through the hotel car park. Not even a tremor. Anyway, better to be safe than buried under a ton of rubble. Besides, I had to be back at the airport by five in the morning for my flight to New York. After we boarded the flight we were told that the weather in New York was bad and we were to hold at source. We stayed for over an hour in the plane, at which point the captain said he had no idea how long we might be grounded.

We were allowed to disembark but told not to wander too far. After a three-hour delay we finally took off. Upon arrival in New York, I found I had missed my British Airways connection to London. There was an alternative flight, though, for which they gave me a new boarding pass and told me to hurry to gate twenty-two. I was at gate one. There was a bus outside where it was raining, how do they say it, cats and dogs. Have you ever wondered where such expressions come from? I've never in my life seen cats and dogs falling from the sky, have you?

Hanging on for dear life to the footboards, as the bus was packed like a commuter bus in New Delhi (you would have to personally experience it to appreciate it), I arrived drenched and dripping at gate twenty-two. The flight was closed and would you believe it, they gave my seat to a standby BA staff member—*an unpaid freeloader*. I would have complained but there was no one at the desk as it was the last flight out for the day and the BA ground-service staff had gone home.

I approached the desk of United Airlines and explained that they brought me here from San Diego and made me miss my BA flight to London. They were efficient and courteous. They offered overnight accommodations in a hotel and rebooked my flight on another BA flight leaving the next morning. They advised me to wait outside the terminal by the curb, as the hotel bus would pick me up in the next ten minutes.

A Japanese gentleman who spoke not a word of English and a young Indian lady who for the first time had come out of India and was visiting her uncle and aunt in the US were also stranded and on their behalf I spoke to the United desk and also got them accommodations at the same hotel. I advised the two—in sign language to the Japanese and in Hindi to the Indian lady—to wait inside while I stood out in the rain for the bus.

It grew dark and I was alone standing by the curb when suddenly a fast-moving Cadillac screeched to a halt and two rather muscle-bound, black guys approached me, one with a knife, and demanded my wallet. How could I refuse? I smiled and handed it over and they left. Still no bus so I went back inside and called the hotel to complain, "I've been robbed and I am cold and have been waiting for over forty minutes. Where the hell is that bus?"

"Please don't shout, sir," a high-pitched voice shouted, "it will be there in the next five, so wait outside."

Back on the sidewalk and the Cadillac approached again and I took off my wedding ring and wristwatch. The tall one ignored my offering and handed back my American Express card, saying, "Hey dude," in a rather friendly manner, "we only take cash and besides, you might need this."

I thanked him for his generosity and he climbed back in his chariot and rolled down his window to shout, "Could we drop you somewhere? It's awfully cold out here."

"Oh no, thank you ever so much," I answered instinctively. I remembered he still had that serrated large blade in his possession. They took off and after about twenty minutes the bus arrived and took all three of us to the hotel, in Queens. There, we found about seventy people queuing up to book a room. By the time my turn came, the reception clerk advised me that no more rooms were available, only the Presidential Suite and it cost $700 for the night. I pulled out my AMEX card and for the first time in my life understood what they mean by—*Never leave home without it.*

It was a large suite with a bedroom and sitting area so I offered the bed to the Indian lady, one sofa to the Japanese gentleman and stretched out on another sofa myself. Suddenly I heard sobbing and then loud weeping from the young maiden, so I asked, "Are you okay?"

In between her sobs she uttered haltingly, "I am going to be gang raped."

And the floodgates opened and tears started to roll down her cheeks.

"Look lady," said I in a soft but irate voice, "I know nothing about the intention of the Japanese gentleman but as for me, I'm bloody exhausted. I've been jolted by a hurricane, shaken by an earthquake, soaked to the bone by cold rain, mugged at knifepoint, and am paying an exorbitant amount of money to spend the night on a sofa. So unless you can offer a cold beer and a hot sandwich, all I am interested in is sleep. Good night."

I slammed her bedroom door shut and wondered if I could find a job where I didn't have to tax my brain and travel wasn't involved. Maybe I could work as a cashier at K-Mart or better still, I could work for Revenue Canada. Little did I know that fate had even more sinister outcome waiting for me back in Arabia that would force me to leve the magic Kingdom and come to a complete circlr by returning to India? But for you to know about it, you would have to spend a few dollars and buy my next book, 'Incredible India'. Untill then, and as they say in Arabia, "*As-Salaam-Alaikum*".

- The End -